50 German Restaurant Bread Recipes for Home

By: Kelly Johnson

Table of Contents

- Bauernbrot
- Pumpernickel
- Roggenmischbrot
- Vollkornbrot
- Zwiebelbrot
- Kartoffelbrot
- Laugenbrot
- Brot mit Sauerteig
- Kürbiskernbrot
- Dinkelbrot
- Ruchbrot
- Kräuterbrot
- Mehrkornbrot
- Bärlauchbrot
- Schwarzbrot
- Roggenbrot
- Brot mit Nüssen
- Apfelbrot
- Weizenmischbrot
- Sonnenblumenkernbrot
- Römisches Brot
- Quarkbrot
- Mohnbrot
- Kastenbrot
- Brezenbrot
- Knäckebrot
- Spelt Bread
- Kümmelbrot
- Bauernlandbrot
- Knoblauchbrot
- Hefezopf
- Poppy Seed Bread

- Butterbrot
- Studentenbrot
- Heidelbeerbrot
- Kaffeebrot
- Walnussbrot
- Roggen-Karotten-Brot
- Baguette Brot
- Schrotbrot
- Roggen-Mehrkornbrot
- Keksbrot
- Pfefferminzbrot
- Joghurtbrot
- Zuckerrübensirupbrot
- Osterbrot
- Apfel-Zimt-Brot
- Essigbrot
- Kürbisbrot
- Rosinenbrot

Bauernbrot

Ingredients:

- **For the Starter:**
    - 1 cup rye flour
    - 1 cup warm water
    - 1/2 teaspoon active dry yeast
- **For the Dough:**
    - 2 1/2 cups all-purpose flour
    - 1 cup whole wheat flour
    - 1 1/2 cups warm water
    - 2 teaspoons salt
    - 1 tablespoon sugar
    - 1 tablespoon olive oil
    - 1 tablespoon active dry yeast

Instructions:

1. **Prepare the Starter:**
    - In a bowl, combine rye flour, warm water, and yeast. Mix well and let it sit for 12-16 hours at room temperature.
2. **Mix the Dough:**
    - In a large bowl, combine all-purpose flour, whole wheat flour, salt, and sugar.
    - In a separate bowl, dissolve yeast in warm water and let it sit for 5 minutes.
    - Add the starter, yeast mixture, and olive oil to the flour mixture. Mix until a dough forms.
3. **Knead the Dough:**
    - Turn the dough onto a floured surface and knead for about 10 minutes, until smooth and elastic.
4. **First Rise:**
    - Place the dough in a lightly oiled bowl, cover with a cloth, and let it rise in a warm place for about 1-2 hours, or until doubled in size.
5. **Shape the Loaf:**
    - Punch down the dough and shape it into a round loaf.
    - Place it on a parchment-lined baking sheet or in a greased loaf pan.
6. **Second Rise:**
    - Cover and let the dough rise for another 30-45 minutes, or until puffy.
7. **Bake:**
    - Preheat the oven to 375°F (190°C).
    - Bake for 35-40 minutes, or until the bread is golden brown and sounds hollow when tapped.

8. **Cool:**
    - Let the bread cool on a wire rack before slicing.

Enjoy your Bauernbrot with butter, cheese, or as a hearty sandwich base!

Pumpernickel

Ingredients:

- **For the Dough:**
    - 2 cups coarsely ground rye flour
    - 1 cup whole rye flour
    - 2 cups warm water (110°F or 45°C)
    - 1 tablespoon active dry yeast
    - 1 tablespoon sugar
    - 1 1/2 teaspoons salt
    - 1/4 cup molasses
    - 1 tablespoon caraway seeds (optional)

Instructions:

1. **Prepare the Yeast Mixture:**
    - In a small bowl, dissolve sugar in warm water. Sprinkle yeast on top and let it sit for 5-10 minutes, until frothy.
2. **Mix the Dough:**
    - In a large bowl, combine coarsely ground rye flour, whole rye flour, and salt.
    - Add the yeast mixture, molasses, and caraway seeds if using. Mix until a thick dough forms.
3. **Knead the Dough:**
    - Turn the dough onto a floured surface and knead for about 5-7 minutes until smooth. Rye dough is dense and sticky, so use minimal flour.
4. **First Rise:**
    - Place the dough in a lightly oiled bowl, cover with a cloth or plastic wrap, and let it rise in a warm, draft-free area for about 1-2 hours, or until doubled in size.
5. **Shape the Loaf:**
    - Punch down the dough and shape it into a loaf. Place it in a greased loaf pan or on a parchment-lined baking sheet.
6. **Second Rise:**
    - Cover and let it rise for another 30-45 minutes.
7. **Bake:**
    - Preheat your oven to 350°F (175°C).
    - Bake for 60-70 minutes, or until the bread is dark brown and sounds hollow when tapped.
8. **Cool:**
    - Allow the bread to cool on a wire rack before slicing.

Pumpernickel is great with butter, cheeses, or as an accompaniment to hearty soups and stews. Enjoy its deep, robust flavor!

Roggenmischbrot

Ingredients:

- **For the Starter:**
    - 1 cup rye flour
    - 1 cup warm water
    - 1/2 teaspoon active dry yeast
- **For the Dough:**
    - 2 cups all-purpose flour
    - 1 cup whole rye flour
    - 1 1/2 cups warm water (110°F or 45°C)
    - 1 tablespoon active dry yeast
    - 1 tablespoon sugar
    - 1 1/2 teaspoons salt
    - 2 tablespoons olive oil or melted butter

Instructions:

1. **Prepare the Starter:**
    - In a bowl, combine rye flour, warm water, and yeast. Mix well and let it sit for 12-16 hours at room temperature.
2. **Mix the Dough:**
    - In a large bowl, combine all-purpose flour, whole rye flour, and salt.
    - In a separate bowl, dissolve sugar in warm water and sprinkle yeast over it. Let it sit for 5 minutes.
    - Add the starter, yeast mixture, and olive oil (or melted butter) to the flour mixture. Mix until a dough forms.
3. **Knead the Dough:**
    - Turn the dough onto a floured surface and knead for about 10 minutes, until smooth and elastic.
4. **First Rise:**
    - Place the dough in a lightly oiled bowl, cover with a cloth or plastic wrap, and let it rise in a warm, draft-free area for about 1-2 hours, or until doubled in size.
5. **Shape the Loaf:**
    - Punch down the dough and turn it out onto a floured surface.
    - Shape into a loaf and place it in a greased loaf pan or on a parchment-lined baking sheet.
6. **Second Rise:**
    - Cover and let the dough rise for another 30-45 minutes, or until puffy.
7. **Bake:**
    - Preheat your oven to 375°F (190°C).
    - Bake the bread for 35-40 minutes, or until golden brown and the bread sounds hollow when tapped.
8. **Cool:**
    - Allow the bread to cool on a wire rack before slicing.

This Roggenmischbrot has a rich, hearty flavor with a nice balance between the tang of rye and the softness of wheat. It's great for sandwiches or as an accompaniment to soups and stews. Enjoy!

Vollkornbrot

Ingredients:

- **For the Dough:**
    - 3 1/2 cups whole grain flour (such as whole wheat or spelt)
    - 1 1/2 cups warm water (110°F or 45°C)
    - 2 tablespoons active dry yeast
    - 1 tablespoon honey or sugar
    - 1 1/2 teaspoons salt
    - 1/4 cup vegetable oil or melted butter
    - Optional: 1/2 cup seeds (such as sunflower, flax, or sesame) or nuts for added texture

Instructions:

1. **Prepare the Yeast Mixture:**
    - In a small bowl, combine warm water and honey (or sugar). Stir to dissolve.
    - Sprinkle the yeast over the mixture and let it sit for 5-10 minutes, until frothy.
2. **Mix the Dough:**
    - In a large bowl, combine whole grain flour and salt.
    - Add the yeast mixture and vegetable oil (or melted butter). Mix until a dough forms.
    - If using, fold in seeds or nuts.
3. **Knead the Dough:**
    - Turn the dough onto a floured surface and knead for about 10 minutes, until smooth and elastic.
4. **First Rise:**
    - Place the dough in a lightly oiled bowl, cover with a cloth or plastic wrap, and let it rise in a warm, draft-free area for about 1-1.5 hours, or until doubled in size.
5. **Shape the Loaf:**
    - Punch down the dough and turn it out onto a floured surface.
    - Shape into a loaf and place it in a greased loaf pan or on a parchment-lined baking sheet.
6. **Second Rise:**
    - Cover and let the dough rise for another 30-45 minutes, or until puffy.
7. **Bake:**
    - Preheat your oven to 375°F (190°C).
    - Bake the bread for 35-40 minutes, or until golden brown and the bread sounds hollow when tapped.
8. **Cool:**
    - Allow the bread to cool on a wire rack before slicing.

Vollkornbrot is hearty and nutritious, perfect for sandwiches or as a satisfying accompaniment to any meal. Enjoy its robust flavor and texture!

Zwiebelbrot

Ingredients:

- **For the Dough:**
    - 3 1/2 cups all-purpose flour
    - 1 1/2 cups warm water (110°F or 45°C)
    - 2 tablespoons active dry yeast
    - 1 tablespoon sugar
    - 1 1/2 teaspoons salt
    - 1/4 cup olive oil or melted butter
- **For the Onions:**
    - 2 large onions, finely chopped
    - 2 tablespoons olive oil
    - 1 teaspoon sugar (to help caramelize)
    - Optional: 1 teaspoon dried thyme or rosemary

Instructions:

1. **Caramelize the Onions:**
    - Heat olive oil in a pan over medium heat. Add onions and sugar.
    - Cook, stirring occasionally, for about 15-20 minutes until onions are golden brown and caramelized. Set aside to cool.
2. **Prepare the Yeast Mixture:**
    - In a small bowl, combine warm water and sugar. Stir to dissolve.
    - Sprinkle the yeast over the mixture and let it sit for 5-10 minutes, until frothy.
3. **Mix the Dough:**
    - In a large bowl, combine flour and salt.
    - Add the yeast mixture and olive oil (or melted butter). Mix until a dough forms.
    - Gently fold in the caramelized onions (and thyme or rosemary if using).
4. **Knead the Dough:**
    - Turn the dough onto a floured surface and knead for about 10 minutes, until smooth and elastic.
5. **First Rise:**
    - Place the dough in a lightly oiled bowl, cover with a cloth or plastic wrap, and let it rise in a warm, draft-free area for about 1-1.5 hours, or until doubled in size.
6. **Shape the Loaf:**
    - Punch down the dough and turn it out onto a floured surface.
    - Shape into a loaf and place it in a greased loaf pan or on a parchment-lined baking sheet.
7. **Second Rise:**
    - Cover and let the dough rise for another 30-45 minutes, or until puffy.

8. **Bake:**
    - Preheat your oven to 375°F (190°C).
    - Bake the bread for 30-35 minutes, or until golden brown and the bread sounds hollow when tapped.
9. **Cool:**
    - Allow the bread to cool on a wire rack before slicing.

Enjoy your Zwiebelbrot warm or toasted, ideal for adding a savory touch to any meal!

Kartoffelbrot

Ingredients:

- **For the Dough:**
    - 1 cup mashed potatoes (about 2 medium potatoes, peeled and boiled)
    - 3 1/2 cups all-purpose flour
    - 1 1/2 cups warm water (110°F or 45°C)
    - 2 tablespoons active dry yeast
    - 1 tablespoon sugar
    - 1 1/2 teaspoons salt
    - 1/4 cup olive oil or melted butter

Instructions:

1. **Prepare the Potatoes:**
    - Peel and chop potatoes, then boil until tender. Drain and mash until smooth. Let the mashed potatoes cool to room temperature.
2. **Prepare the Yeast Mixture:**
    - In a small bowl, combine warm water and sugar. Stir to dissolve.
    - Sprinkle the yeast over the mixture and let it sit for 5-10 minutes, until frothy.
3. **Mix the Dough:**
    - In a large bowl, combine flour and salt.
    - Add the yeast mixture, mashed potatoes, and olive oil (or melted butter). Mix until a dough forms.
4. **Knead the Dough:**
    - Turn the dough onto a floured surface and knead for about 8-10 minutes, until smooth and elastic.
5. **First Rise:**
    - Place the dough in a lightly oiled bowl, cover with a cloth or plastic wrap, and let it rise in a warm, draft-free area for about 1-1.5 hours, or until doubled in size.
6. **Shape the Loaf:**
    - Punch down the dough and turn it out onto a floured surface.
    - Shape into a loaf and place it in a greased loaf pan or on a parchment-lined baking sheet.
7. **Second Rise:**
    - Cover and let the dough rise for another 30-45 minutes, or until puffy.
8. **Bake:**
    - Preheat your oven to 375°F (190°C).
    - Bake for 30-35 minutes, or until golden brown and the bread sounds hollow when tapped.
9. **Cool:**

- Allow the bread to cool on a wire rack before slicing.

Kartoffelbrot is delightfully soft and slightly sweet, making it perfect for sandwiches or served with butter. Enjoy!

Laugenbrot

Ingredients:

- **For the Dough:**
    - 3 1/2 cups all-purpose flour
    - 1 1/2 cups warm water (110°F or 45°C)
    - 2 tablespoons active dry yeast
    - 1 tablespoon sugar
    - 1 1/2 teaspoons salt
    - 2 tablespoons olive oil
- **For the Lye Bath:**
    - 1/4 cup food-grade lye (sodium hydroxide)
    - 4 cups water
- **For Topping:**
    - Coarse sea salt (optional)

Instructions:

1. **Prepare the Dough:**
    - In a small bowl, dissolve sugar in warm water and sprinkle yeast on top. Let it sit for 5-10 minutes, until frothy.
    - In a large bowl, combine flour and salt.
    - Add the yeast mixture and olive oil to the flour. Mix until a dough forms.
2. **Knead the Dough:**
    - Turn the dough onto a floured surface and knead for about 8-10 minutes, until smooth and elastic.
3. **First Rise:**
    - Place the dough in a lightly oiled bowl, cover with a cloth or plastic wrap, and let it rise in a warm, draft-free area for about 1-1.5 hours, or until doubled in size.
4. **Shape the Loaf:**
    - Punch down the dough and turn it out onto a floured surface. Shape into a loaf or desired shape.
    - Place the shaped dough on a parchment-lined baking sheet.
5. **Prepare the Lye Bath:**
    - Wear gloves and safety goggles. In a well-ventilated area, carefully dissolve lye in water. (Note: Handle lye with caution, as it is a caustic substance.)
    - Using a slotted spoon, carefully dip the dough into the lye bath for about 20-30 seconds, then place it back on the baking sheet. If desired, sprinkle with coarse sea salt.
6. **Second Rise:**
    - Let the dough rise for another 30 minutes.

7. **Bake:**
     - Preheat your oven to 425°F (220°C).
     - Bake the bread for 25-30 minutes, or until dark brown and the bread sounds hollow when tapped.
8. **Cool:**
     - Allow the bread to cool on a wire rack before slicing.

Laugenbrot has a signature chewy crust and a rich flavor. It's often enjoyed with mustard or as a hearty sandwich base. Enjoy!

Brot mit Sauerteig

Ingredients:

- **For the Starter:**
    - 1 cup all-purpose flour
    - 1/2 cup water
    - 1 tablespoon active sourdough starter (or use a store-bought starter)
- **For the Dough:**
    - 3 cups all-purpose flour
    - 1 1/2 cups warm water (110°F or 45°C)
    - 1 1/2 teaspoons salt
    - 1 cup sourdough starter (prepared and active)

Instructions:

1. **Prepare the Starter (If Not Using a Pre-made Starter):**
    - Combine 1 cup flour and 1/2 cup water in a jar. Mix well.
    - Cover loosely and let it sit at room temperature for 24 hours.
    - Feed the starter daily by discarding half and adding 1/2 cup flour and 1/4 cup water until it becomes bubbly and active (about 5-7 days).
2. **Mix the Dough:**
    - In a large bowl, combine flour and salt.
    - Add the sourdough starter and warm water. Mix until a dough forms.
3. **Knead the Dough:**
    - Turn the dough onto a floured surface and knead for about 10 minutes, until smooth and elastic.
4. **First Rise:**
    - Place the dough in a lightly oiled bowl, cover with a cloth or plastic wrap, and let it rise at room temperature for 4-6 hours, or until doubled in size.
5. **Shape the Loaf:**
    - Punch down the dough and turn it out onto a floured surface.
    - Shape into a round or oval loaf and place it on a parchment-lined baking sheet or into a floured proofing basket.
6. **Second Rise:**
    - Cover and let the dough rise for another 2-3 hours, or until puffy.
7. **Preheat the Oven:**
    - Preheat your oven to 450°F (230°C).
8. **Score and Bake:**
    - Just before baking, use a sharp knife to score the top of the loaf.
    - Bake for 30-35 minutes, or until the bread is golden brown and sounds hollow when tapped.
9. **Cool:**

- Allow the bread to cool on a wire rack before slicing.

Sourdough bread has a chewy crust and tangy flavor, perfect for sandwiches or enjoyed on its own. Enjoy!

Kürbiskernbrot

Ingredients:

- **For the Dough:**
    - 3 1/2 cups all-purpose flour or bread flour
    - 1 cup whole wheat flour
    - 1 1/2 cups warm water (110°F or 45°C)
    - 2 tablespoons active dry yeast
    - 1 tablespoon sugar
    - 1 1/2 teaspoons salt
    - 1/4 cup olive oil or melted butter
    - 1 cup pumpkin seeds (plus extra for topping)

Instructions:

1. **Prepare the Yeast Mixture:**
    - In a small bowl, combine warm water and sugar. Stir to dissolve.
    - Sprinkle the yeast over the mixture and let it sit for 5-10 minutes, until frothy.
2. **Mix the Dough:**
    - In a large bowl, combine all-purpose flour, whole wheat flour, and salt.
    - Add the yeast mixture and olive oil (or melted butter). Mix until a dough forms.
3. **Add Pumpkin Seeds:**
    - Gently fold in the pumpkin seeds, mixing until evenly distributed.
4. **Knead the Dough:**
    - Turn the dough onto a floured surface and knead for about 8-10 minutes, until smooth and elastic.
5. **First Rise:**
    - Place the dough in a lightly oiled bowl, cover with a cloth or plastic wrap, and let it rise in a warm, draft-free area for about 1-1.5 hours, or until doubled in size.
6. **Shape the Loaf:**
    - Punch down the dough and turn it out onto a floured surface.
    - Shape the dough into a loaf or divide it into smaller loaves.
    - Place the shaped dough on a parchment-lined baking sheet or in greased loaf pans.
    - Optionally, sprinkle additional pumpkin seeds on top of the dough and press them in lightly.
7. **Second Rise:**
    - Cover and let the dough rise for another 30-45 minutes, or until puffy.
8. **Bake:**
    - Preheat your oven to 375°F (190°C).

- Bake for 30-35 minutes, or until the bread is golden brown and sounds hollow when tapped.
9. **Cool:**
    - Allow the bread to cool on a wire rack before slicing.

Kürbiskernbrot is perfect for sandwiches, served with cheese, or enjoyed with a spread. Its crunchy texture and nutty flavor make it a delightful addition to any meal. Enjoy!

Dinkelbrot

Ingredients:

- **For the Dough:**
    - 3 1/2 cups spelt flour
    - 1 1/2 cups warm water (110°F or 45°C)
    - 2 tablespoons active dry yeast
    - 1 tablespoon honey or sugar
    - 1 1/2 teaspoons salt
    - 1/4 cup olive oil or melted butter

Instructions:

1. **Prepare the Yeast Mixture:**
    - In a small bowl, combine warm water and honey (or sugar). Stir to dissolve.
    - Sprinkle the yeast over the mixture and let it sit for 5-10 minutes, until frothy.
2. **Mix the Dough:**
    - In a large bowl, combine spelt flour and salt.
    - Add the yeast mixture and olive oil (or melted butter). Mix until a dough forms.
3. **Knead the Dough:**
    - Turn the dough onto a floured surface and knead for about 8-10 minutes, until smooth and elastic.
4. **First Rise:**
    - Place the dough in a lightly oiled bowl, cover with a cloth or plastic wrap, and let it rise in a warm, draft-free area for about 1-1.5 hours, or until doubled in size.
5. **Shape the Loaf:**
    - Punch down the dough and turn it out onto a floured surface.
    - Shape into a loaf and place it in a greased loaf pan or on a parchment-lined baking sheet.
6. **Second Rise:**
    - Cover and let the dough rise for another 30-45 minutes, or until puffy.
7. **Bake:**
    - Preheat your oven to 375°F (190°C).
    - Bake for 30-35 minutes, or until golden brown and the bread sounds hollow when tapped.
8. **Cool:**
    - Allow the bread to cool on a wire rack before slicing.

Dinkelbrot is great for sandwiches, toast, or simply enjoyed with butter. Its mild, nutty flavor makes it a versatile addition to any meal. Enjoy!

Ruchbrot

Ingredients:

- **For the Dough:**
    - 3 cups bread flour
    - 1 cup whole wheat flour
    - 1 cup warm water (110°F or 45°C)
    - 2 tablespoons active dry yeast
    - 1 tablespoon sugar
    - 1 1/2 teaspoons salt
    - 2 tablespoons olive oil or melted butter

Instructions:

1. **Prepare the Yeast Mixture:**
    - In a small bowl, dissolve sugar in warm water. Sprinkle yeast on top and let it sit for 5-10 minutes, until frothy.
2. **Mix the Dough:**
    - In a large bowl, combine bread flour, whole wheat flour, and salt.
    - Add the yeast mixture and olive oil (or melted butter). Mix until a dough forms.
3. **Knead the Dough:**
    - Turn the dough onto a floured surface and knead for about 8-10 minutes, until smooth and elastic.
4. **First Rise:**
    - Place the dough in a lightly oiled bowl, cover with a cloth or plastic wrap, and let it rise in a warm, draft-free area for about 1-1.5 hours, or until doubled in size.
5. **Shape the Loaf:**
    - Punch down the dough and turn it out onto a floured surface.
    - Shape into a loaf and place it in a greased loaf pan or on a parchment-lined baking sheet.
6. **Second Rise:**
    - Cover and let the dough rise for another 30-45 minutes, or until puffy.
7. **Bake:**
    - Preheat your oven to 375°F (190°C).
    - Bake for 30-35 minutes, or until the bread is golden brown and sounds hollow when tapped.
8. **Cool:**
    - Allow the bread to cool on a wire rack before slicing.

Ruchbrot has a robust flavor and chewy texture, making it perfect for sandwiches, spreads, or as an accompaniment to soups and stews. Enjoy!

Kräuterbrot

Ingredients:

- **For the Dough:**
    - 3 1/2 cups all-purpose flour
    - 1 1/2 cups warm water (110°F or 45°C)
    - 2 tablespoons active dry yeast
    - 1 tablespoon sugar
    - 1 1/2 teaspoons salt
    - 1/4 cup olive oil
- **For the Herbs:**
    - 2 tablespoons chopped fresh parsley (or 2 teaspoons dried)
    - 2 tablespoons chopped fresh chives (or 2 teaspoons dried)
    - 1 tablespoon chopped fresh rosemary (or 1 teaspoon dried)
    - Optional: 1 teaspoon dried thyme or basil

Instructions:

1. **Prepare the Yeast Mixture:**
    - In a small bowl, combine warm water and sugar. Stir to dissolve.
    - Sprinkle yeast over the mixture and let it sit for 5-10 minutes, until frothy.
2. **Mix the Dough:**
    - In a large bowl, combine flour and salt.
    - Add the yeast mixture, olive oil, and chopped herbs. Mix until a dough forms.
3. **Knead the Dough:**
    - Turn the dough onto a floured surface and knead for about 8-10 minutes, until smooth and elastic.
4. **First Rise:**
    - Place the dough in a lightly oiled bowl, cover with a cloth or plastic wrap, and let it rise in a warm, draft-free area for about 1-1.5 hours, or until doubled in size.
5. **Shape the Loaf:**
    - Punch down the dough and turn it out onto a floured surface.
    - Shape into a loaf or divide into smaller loaves and place them on a parchment-lined baking sheet.
6. **Second Rise:**
    - Cover and let the dough rise for another 30-45 minutes, or until puffy.
7. **Bake:**
    - Preheat your oven to 375°F (190°C).
    - Bake for 30-35 minutes, or until the bread is golden brown and sounds hollow when tapped.
8. **Cool:**
    - Allow the bread to cool on a wire rack before slicing.

Kräuterbrot is aromatic and versatile, perfect for adding a burst of flavor to any meal. Enjoy it with cheese, soups, or just a bit of butter!

Mehrkornbrot

Ingredients:

- **For the Dough:**
    - 2 1/2 cups all-purpose flour
    - 1 cup whole wheat flour
    - 1/2 cup rolled oats
    - 1/4 cup sunflower seeds
    - 1/4 cup flaxseeds
    - 1/4 cup sesame seeds
    - 1 1/2 cups warm water (110°F or 45°C)
    - 2 tablespoons active dry yeast
    - 1 tablespoon honey or sugar
    - 1 1/2 teaspoons salt
    - 1/4 cup vegetable oil or melted butter

Instructions:

1. **Prepare the Yeast Mixture:**
    - In a small bowl, combine warm water and honey (or sugar). Stir to dissolve.
    - Sprinkle the yeast over the mixture and let it sit for 5-10 minutes, until frothy.
2. **Mix the Dough:**
    - In a large bowl, combine all-purpose flour, whole wheat flour, salt, rolled oats, sunflower seeds, flaxseeds, and sesame seeds.
    - Add the yeast mixture and vegetable oil (or melted butter). Mix until a dough forms.
3. **Knead the Dough:**
    - Turn the dough onto a floured surface and knead for about 8-10 minutes, until smooth and elastic.
4. **First Rise:**
    - Place the dough in a lightly oiled bowl, cover with a cloth or plastic wrap, and let it rise in a warm, draft-free area for about 1-1.5 hours, or until doubled in size.
5. **Shape the Loaf:**
    - Punch down the dough and turn it out onto a floured surface.
    - Shape into a loaf and place it in a greased loaf pan or on a parchment-lined baking sheet.
6. **Second Rise:**
    - Cover and let the dough rise for another 30-45 minutes, or until puffy.
7. **Bake:**
    - Preheat your oven to 375°F (190°C).

- Bake for 30-35 minutes, or until the bread is golden brown and sounds hollow when tapped.
8. **Cool:**
    - Allow the bread to cool on a wire rack before slicing.

Mehrkornbrot is hearty and filling, with a satisfying crunch from the seeds and a chewy texture. It's great for sandwiches, toast, or as an accompaniment to soups and salads. Enjoy your multi-grain creation!

Bärlauchbrot

Ingredients:

- **For the Dough:**
    - 3 1/2 cups all-purpose flour
    - 1 1/2 cups warm water (110°F or 45°C)
    - 2 tablespoons active dry yeast
    - 1 tablespoon sugar
    - 1 1/2 teaspoons salt
    - 1/4 cup olive oil
- **For the Wild Garlic Mixture:**
    - 1 cup fresh wild garlic leaves, finely chopped (or 1/2 cup garlic chives, finely chopped)
    - 2 tablespoons olive oil
    - Optional: 1 tablespoon chopped fresh parsley

Instructions:

1. **Prepare the Yeast Mixture:**
    - In a small bowl, combine warm water and sugar. Stir to dissolve.
    - Sprinkle the yeast over the mixture and let it sit for 5-10 minutes, until frothy.
2. **Prepare the Wild Garlic Mixture:**
    - In a small bowl, combine chopped wild garlic with olive oil. If using, add parsley for extra flavor. Set aside.
3. **Mix the Dough:**
    - In a large bowl, combine flour and salt.
    - Add the yeast mixture and olive oil. Mix until a dough forms.
4. **Knead the Dough:**
    - Turn the dough onto a floured surface and knead for about 8-10 minutes, until smooth and elastic.
5. **Incorporate the Wild Garlic:**
    - Gently fold the wild garlic mixture into the dough, ensuring it's evenly distributed.
6. **First Rise:**
    - Place the dough in a lightly oiled bowl, cover with a cloth or plastic wrap, and let it rise in a warm, draft-free area for about 1-1.5 hours, or until doubled in size.
7. **Shape the Loaf:**
    - Punch down the dough and turn it out onto a floured surface.
    - Shape into a loaf or divide into smaller loaves. Place on a parchment-lined baking sheet or into greased loaf pans.
8. **Second Rise:**
    - Cover and let the dough rise for another 30-45 minutes, or until puffy.

9. **Bake:**
    - Preheat your oven to 375°F (190°C).
    - Bake for 30-35 minutes, or until the bread is golden brown and sounds hollow when tapped.
10. **Cool:**
    - Allow the bread to cool on a wire rack before slicing.

Bärlauchbrot has a delightful, savory aroma and flavor that pairs wonderfully with cheeses, soups, or simply enjoyed with butter. Enjoy your fresh, herb-infused bread!

Schwarzbrot

Ingredients:

- **For the Dough:**
    - 2 1/2 cups rye flour
    - 1 1/2 cups all-purpose flour
    - 1 1/2 cups warm water (110°F or 45°C)
    - 1/2 cup sourdough starter (active and bubbly; you can also use store-bought)
    - 2 tablespoons active dry yeast
    - 1 tablespoon sugar
    - 1 tablespoon caraway seeds (optional, but traditional)
    - 1 1/2 teaspoons salt
    - 1/4 cup molasses or dark honey

Instructions:

1. **Prepare the Yeast Mixture:**
    - In a small bowl, combine warm water and sugar. Stir to dissolve.
    - Sprinkle the yeast over the mixture and let it sit for 5-10 minutes, until frothy.
2. **Mix the Dough:**
    - In a large bowl, combine rye flour, all-purpose flour, caraway seeds (if using), and salt.
    - Add the yeast mixture, sourdough starter, and molasses. Mix until a dough forms.
3. **Knead the Dough:**
    - Turn the dough onto a floured surface and knead for about 10 minutes, until smooth and elastic. Note that rye dough is typically stickier and denser than wheat dough.
4. **First Rise:**
    - Place the dough in a lightly oiled bowl, cover with a cloth or plastic wrap, and let it rise in a warm, draft-free area for about 1-1.5 hours, or until doubled in size.
5. **Shape the Loaf:**
    - Punch down the dough and turn it out onto a floured surface.
    - Shape into a loaf or divide into smaller loaves. Place on a parchment-lined baking sheet or in greased loaf pans.
6. **Second Rise:**
    - Cover and let the dough rise for another 30-45 minutes, or until puffy.
7. **Preheat the Oven:**
    - Preheat your oven to 375°F (190°C).
8. **Bake:**
    - Bake the bread for 35-40 minutes, or until the bread is deep brown and sounds hollow when tapped.

9. **Cool:**
   - Allow the bread to cool on a wire rack before slicing.

Tips:

- **For a More Traditional Flavor:** Use a rye sourdough starter and let the dough ferment for a longer period for a deeper flavor.
- **Texture:** If the dough seems too sticky, you can add a bit more flour as needed, but be careful not to overdo it as rye flour doesn't handle as much flour as wheat flour.

Schwarzbrot is perfect for hearty sandwiches, or enjoyed with cold cuts, cheeses, or simply with butter. Its robust flavor and dense crumb make it a staple in German cuisine. Enjoy!

Roggenbrot

Ingredients:

- **For the Dough:**
    - 2 1/2 cups rye flour
    - 1 cup all-purpose flour
    - 1 1/2 cups warm water (110°F or 45°C)
    - 2 tablespoons active dry yeast
    - 1 tablespoon honey or sugar
    - 1 1/2 teaspoons salt
    - 1/4 cup caraway seeds (optional, for traditional flavor)
- **For the Sourdough Starter (Optional, for added flavor):**
    - 1/2 cup rye flour
    - 1/2 cup water
    - 1 tablespoon active sourdough starter or a pinch of yeast

Instructions:

1. **Prepare the Sourdough Starter (Optional):**
    - If using a sourdough starter, mix 1/2 cup rye flour and 1/2 cup water in a bowl. Stir to combine.
    - Cover loosely and let it sit at room temperature for 24-48 hours, feeding it daily with equal parts flour and water, until bubbly and active. If using a pre-made starter, you can skip this step.
2. **Prepare the Yeast Mixture:**
    - In a small bowl, combine warm water and honey (or sugar). Stir to dissolve.
    - Sprinkle yeast over the mixture and let it sit for 5-10 minutes, until frothy.
3. **Mix the Dough:**
    - In a large bowl, combine rye flour, all-purpose flour, salt, and caraway seeds (if using).
    - Add the yeast mixture and sourdough starter (if using). Mix until a dough forms.
4. **Knead the Dough:**
    - Turn the dough onto a floured surface and knead for about 8-10 minutes. Rye dough is generally stickier and denser, so you may need to add a little more flour if it's too sticky.
5. **First Rise:**
    - Place the dough in a lightly oiled bowl, cover with a cloth or plastic wrap, and let it rise in a warm, draft-free area for about 1-1.5 hours, or until doubled in size.
6. **Shape the Loaf:**
    - Punch down the dough and turn it out onto a floured surface.

- Shape into a loaf and place on a parchment-lined baking sheet or in a greased loaf pan.
7. **Second Rise:**
    - Cover and let the dough rise for another 30-45 minutes, or until puffy.
8. **Preheat the Oven:**
    - Preheat your oven to 375°F (190°C).
9. **Bake:**
    - Bake the bread for 35-40 minutes, or until it's deep brown and sounds hollow when tapped on the bottom.
10. **Cool:**
    - Allow the bread to cool on a wire rack before slicing.

Tips:

- **For Extra Flavor:** Adding a tablespoon of malt extract or dark molasses can enhance the bread's flavor and color.
- **For a Traditional Crust:** Place a small pan of water in the oven while baking to create steam, which helps develop a crustier exterior.

Roggenbrot is excellent for making hearty sandwiches, and it pairs well with a variety of toppings, from cheeses to cold cuts. Enjoy your delicious, homemade rye bread!

Brot mit Nüssen

Ingredients:

- **For the Dough:**
    - 3 1/2 cups all-purpose flour
    - 1 cup whole wheat flour
    - 1 1/2 cups warm water (110°F or 45°C)
    - 2 tablespoons active dry yeast
    - 1 tablespoon honey or sugar
    - 1 1/2 teaspoons salt
    - 1/4 cup olive oil or melted butter
- **For the Nuts:**
    - 1/2 cup walnuts, chopped
    - 1/2 cup almonds, chopped
    - 1/4 cup sunflower seeds (optional)
    - 1/4 cup hazelnuts, chopped (optional)

Instructions:

1. **Prepare the Yeast Mixture:**
    - In a small bowl, combine warm water and honey (or sugar). Stir to dissolve.
    - Sprinkle the yeast over the mixture and let it sit for 5-10 minutes, until frothy.
2. **Mix the Dough:**
    - In a large bowl, combine all-purpose flour, whole wheat flour, and salt.
    - Add the yeast mixture and olive oil (or melted butter). Mix until a dough forms.
3. **Incorporate the Nuts:**
    - Gently fold in the chopped walnuts, almonds, sunflower seeds, and hazelnuts until evenly distributed throughout the dough.
4. **Knead the Dough:**
    - Turn the dough onto a floured surface and knead for about 8-10 minutes, until smooth and elastic.
5. **First Rise:**
    - Place the dough in a lightly oiled bowl, cover with a cloth or plastic wrap, and let it rise in a warm, draft-free area for about 1-1.5 hours, or until doubled in size.
6. **Shape the Loaf:**
    - Punch down the dough and turn it out onto a floured surface.
    - Shape into a loaf or divide into smaller loaves. Place on a parchment-lined baking sheet or in greased loaf pans.
7. **Second Rise:**
    - Cover and let the dough rise for another 30-45 minutes, or until puffy.
8. **Preheat the Oven:**

        - Preheat your oven to 375°F (190°C).
9. **Bake:**
        - Bake the bread for 35-40 minutes, or until it is golden brown and sounds hollow when tapped on the bottom.
10. **Cool:**
        - Allow the bread to cool on a wire rack before slicing.

Tips:

- **Nut Variations:** Feel free to use your favorite nuts or a mix of nuts, depending on what you have on hand.
- **Texture:** If you prefer a finer texture, you can chop the nuts more finely or even toast them lightly before adding them to the dough for extra flavor.

Brot mit Nüssen offers a delightful crunch and nutty taste, making it a versatile addition to any meal. It pairs well with cheeses, spreads, or just a pat of butter. Enjoy your homemade nut bread!

Apfelbrot

Ingredients:

- **For the Dough:**
    - 2 1/2 cups all-purpose flour
    - 1/2 cup whole wheat flour
    - 1/2 cup granulated sugar
    - 1 tablespoon baking powder
    - 1/2 teaspoon salt
    - 1 teaspoon ground cinnamon
    - 1/2 teaspoon ground nutmeg (optional)
- **For the Apple Mixture:**
    - 1 cup peeled and chopped apples (about 1 medium apple)
    - 1/4 cup melted butter or vegetable oil
    - 2 large eggs
    - 1/2 cup milk
    - 1 teaspoon vanilla extract
- **Optional:**
    - 1/4 cup chopped nuts (e.g., walnuts or pecans) or raisins for added texture

Instructions:

1. **Prepare the Oven:**
    - Preheat your oven to 350°F (175°C). Grease a loaf pan or line it with parchment paper.
2. **Mix Dry Ingredients:**
    - In a large bowl, whisk together flour, sugar, baking powder, salt, cinnamon, and nutmeg.
3. **Prepare the Apple Mixture:**
    - In another bowl, combine the chopped apples, melted butter (or oil), eggs, milk, and vanilla extract.
4. **Combine Ingredients:**
    - Fold the wet ingredients into the dry ingredients until just combined. Be careful not to overmix.
    - If using, fold in nuts or raisins.
5. **Transfer to Pan:**
    - Pour the batter into the prepared loaf pan and spread it evenly.
6. **Bake:**
    - Bake for 50-60 minutes, or until a toothpick inserted into the center comes out clean.
7. **Cool:**

- Let the bread cool in the pan for about 10 minutes, then transfer it to a wire rack to cool completely before slicing.

Tips:

- **Apple Choice:** Use firm, tart apples like Granny Smith for the best texture and flavor.
- **Spices:** Adjust the spices according to your taste or add a bit of clove for extra warmth.

Apfelbrot is perfect with a cup of tea or coffee, and its moist texture and apple flavor make it a comforting choice for any time of day. Enjoy your homemade apple bread!

Weizenmischbrot

Ingredients:

- **For the Dough:**
    - 2 1/2 cups all-purpose flour
    - 1 cup rye flour
    - 1 1/2 cups warm water (110°F or 45°C)
    - 2 tablespoons active dry yeast
    - 1 tablespoon honey or sugar
    - 1 1/2 teaspoons salt
    - 1/4 cup olive oil or melted butter

Instructions:

1. **Prepare the Yeast Mixture:**
    - In a small bowl, combine warm water and honey (or sugar). Stir to dissolve.
    - Sprinkle the yeast over the mixture and let it sit for 5-10 minutes, until frothy.
2. **Mix the Dough:**
    - In a large bowl, combine all-purpose flour, rye flour, and salt.
    - Add the yeast mixture and olive oil (or melted butter). Mix until a dough forms.
3. **Knead the Dough:**
    - Turn the dough onto a floured surface and knead for about 8-10 minutes, until smooth and elastic.
4. **First Rise:**
    - Place the dough in a lightly oiled bowl, cover with a cloth or plastic wrap, and let it rise in a warm, draft-free area for about 1-1.5 hours, or until doubled in size.
5. **Shape the Loaf:**
    - Punch down the dough and turn it out onto a floured surface.
    - Shape into a loaf and place it on a parchment-lined baking sheet or in a greased loaf pan.
6. **Second Rise:**
    - Cover and let the dough rise for another 30-45 minutes, or until puffy.
7. **Preheat the Oven:**
    - Preheat your oven to 375°F (190°C).
8. **Bake:**
    - Bake for 30-35 minutes, or until the bread is golden brown and sounds hollow when tapped on the bottom.
9. **Cool:**
    - Allow the bread to cool on a wire rack before slicing.

Tips:

- **Texture:** For a crustier crust, place a small pan of water in the oven while baking to create steam.
- **Flavor:** Adding a tablespoon of caraway seeds or sunflower seeds to the dough can enhance the flavor and add texture.

Weizenmischbrot is versatile and pairs well with a variety of toppings, from cheeses to cold cuts. Its balanced flavor and slightly chewy texture make it a favorite in many households. Enjoy your homemade mixed bread!

Sonnenblumenkernbrot

Ingredients:

- **For the Dough:**
    - 3 cups all-purpose flour
    - 1 cup whole wheat flour
    - 1 1/2 cups warm water (110°F or 45°C)
    - 2 tablespoons active dry yeast
    - 1 tablespoon honey or sugar
    - 1 1/2 teaspoons salt
    - 1/4 cup olive oil or melted butter
    - 1/2 cup sunflower seeds (plus extra for topping)

Instructions:

1. **Prepare the Yeast Mixture:**
    - In a small bowl, combine warm water and honey (or sugar). Stir to dissolve.
    - Sprinkle the yeast over the mixture and let it sit for 5-10 minutes, until frothy.
2. **Mix the Dough:**
    - In a large bowl, combine all-purpose flour, whole wheat flour, and salt.
    - Add the yeast mixture and olive oil (or melted butter). Mix until a dough forms.
3. **Incorporate the Sunflower Seeds:**
    - Gently fold in 1/2 cup of sunflower seeds until evenly distributed throughout the dough.
4. **Knead the Dough:**
    - Turn the dough onto a floured surface and knead for about 8-10 minutes, until smooth and elastic.
5. **First Rise:**
    - Place the dough in a lightly oiled bowl, cover with a cloth or plastic wrap, and let it rise in a warm, draft-free area for about 1-1.5 hours, or until doubled in size.
6. **Shape the Loaf:**
    - Punch down the dough and turn it out onto a floured surface.
    - Shape into a loaf and place on a parchment-lined baking sheet or in a greased loaf pan.
    - Sprinkle additional sunflower seeds on top, pressing them lightly into the dough.
7. **Second Rise:**
    - Cover and let the dough rise for another 30-45 minutes, or until puffy.
8. **Preheat the Oven:**
    - Preheat your oven to 375°F (190°C).
9. **Bake:**

- Bake for 35-40 minutes, or until the bread is golden brown and sounds hollow when tapped on the bottom.
10. **Cool:**
    - Allow the bread to cool on a wire rack before slicing.

Tips:

- **Sunflower Seed Variations:** You can toast the sunflower seeds lightly before adding them for extra flavor.
- **Texture:** If you prefer a crustier loaf, place a small pan of water in the oven to create steam during baking.

Sonnenblumenkernbrot is flavorful and satisfying, with a delightful crunch from the sunflower seeds. Enjoy it fresh, toasted, or with your favorite spreads!

Römisches Brot

Ingredients:

- **For the Dough:**
    - 3 1/2 cups all-purpose flour
    - 1 1/2 cups warm water (110°F or 45°C)
    - 2 tablespoons active dry yeast (or 1 packet)
    - 1 tablespoon honey or sugar
    - 1 1/2 teaspoons salt
    - 2 tablespoons olive oil

Instructions:

1. **Prepare the Yeast Mixture:**
    - In a small bowl, combine warm water and honey (or sugar). Stir to dissolve.
    - Sprinkle the yeast over the mixture and let it sit for 5-10 minutes, until frothy.
2. **Mix the Dough:**
    - In a large bowl, combine the flour and salt.
    - Add the yeast mixture and olive oil. Mix until a dough forms.
3. **Knead the Dough:**
    - Turn the dough onto a floured surface and knead for about 8-10 minutes, until smooth and elastic.
4. **First Rise:**
    - Place the dough in a lightly oiled bowl, cover with a cloth or plastic wrap, and let it rise in a warm, draft-free area for about 1-1.5 hours, or until doubled in size.
5. **Shape the Loaf:**
    - Punch down the dough and turn it out onto a floured surface.
    - Shape into a loaf or divide into smaller loaves. Place on a parchment-lined baking sheet or in greased loaf pans.
6. **Second Rise:**
    - Cover and let the dough rise for another 30-45 minutes, or until puffy.
7. **Preheat the Oven:**
    - Preheat your oven to 375°F (190°C).
8. **Bake:**
    - Bake for 30-35 minutes, or until the bread is golden brown and sounds hollow when tapped on the bottom.
9. **Cool:**
    - Allow the bread to cool on a wire rack before slicing.

Tips:

- **For a More Authentic Flavor:** You can add herbs like rosemary or thyme to the dough for a flavor reminiscent of ancient Roman breads.
- **Texture:** For a crustier bread, place a small pan of water in the oven while baking to create steam.

Römisches Brot is a simple, classic bread that pairs well with a variety of dishes, from soups and stews to cheese and olives. Enjoy this slice of history with your meals!

Quarkbrot

Ingredients:

- **For the Dough:**
    - 2 1/2 cups all-purpose flour
    - 1 cup quark (you can substitute with Greek yogurt or cottage cheese if needed)
    - 1 cup warm milk (110°F or 45°C)
    - 1/4 cup olive oil or melted butter
    - 2 tablespoons sugar or honey
    - 2 teaspoons active dry yeast
    - 1 teaspoon salt
    - 1 egg (optional, for added richness)

Instructions:

1. **Prepare the Yeast Mixture:**
    - In a small bowl, combine warm milk and sugar (or honey). Stir to dissolve.
    - Sprinkle the yeast over the mixture and let it sit for 5-10 minutes, until frothy.
2. **Mix the Dough:**
    - In a large bowl, combine flour and salt.
    - Add the quark, olive oil (or melted butter), and the yeast mixture. If using, beat in the egg.
    - Mix until a dough forms.
3. **Knead the Dough:**
    - Turn the dough onto a floured surface and knead for about 8-10 minutes, until smooth and elastic.
4. **First Rise:**
    - Place the dough in a lightly oiled bowl, cover with a cloth or plastic wrap, and let it rise in a warm, draft-free area for about 1-1.5 hours, or until doubled in size.
5. **Shape the Loaf:**
    - Punch down the dough and turn it out onto a floured surface.
    - Shape into a loaf or divide into smaller loaves. Place on a parchment-lined baking sheet or in greased loaf pans.
6. **Second Rise:**
    - Cover and let the dough rise for another 30-45 minutes, or until puffy.
7. **Preheat the Oven:**
    - Preheat your oven to 375°F (190°C).
8. **Bake:**
    - Bake for 30-35 minutes, or until the bread is golden brown and sounds hollow when tapped on the bottom.
9. **Cool:**

- Allow the bread to cool on a wire rack before slicing.

Tips:

- **Texture:** Quark adds moisture, so if the dough is too sticky, add a bit more flour as needed.
- **Flavor Variations:** You can mix in herbs, cheese, or nuts for additional flavor.

Quarkbrot is versatile and can be enjoyed fresh, toasted, or with a variety of spreads. Its tender crumb and slightly tangy flavor make it a delicious addition to any meal. Enjoy your homemade quark bread!

Mohnbrot

Ingredients:

- **For the Dough:**
    - 3 1/2 cups all-purpose flour
    - 1 cup warm milk (110°F or 45°C)
    - 1/4 cup sugar
    - 1/4 cup melted butter or vegetable oil
    - 2 teaspoons active dry yeast (or 1 packet)
    - 1 teaspoon salt
    - 1 large egg (optional, for added richness)
- **For the Poppy Seed Filling:**
    - 1/2 cup poppy seeds
    - 1/2 cup milk
    - 1/4 cup sugar
    - 1 tablespoon honey or light corn syrup
    - 1/2 teaspoon vanilla extract (optional)
- **For the Topping (optional):**
    - 2 tablespoons poppy seeds
    - 1 egg, beaten (for egg wash)

Instructions:

1. **Prepare the Yeast Mixture:**
    - In a small bowl, combine warm milk and sugar. Stir to dissolve.
    - Sprinkle the yeast over the mixture and let it sit for 5-10 minutes, until frothy.
2. **Prepare the Poppy Seed Filling:**
    - In a small saucepan, combine poppy seeds, milk, sugar, and honey (or corn syrup). Heat over medium heat, stirring occasionally, until the mixture thickens (about 5-7 minutes). Remove from heat and let cool. Stir in vanilla extract if using.
3. **Mix the Dough:**
    - In a large bowl, combine flour and salt.
    - Add the yeast mixture, melted butter (or oil), and egg (if using). Mix until a dough forms.
4. **Knead the Dough:**
    - Turn the dough onto a floured surface and knead for about 8-10 minutes, until smooth and elastic.
5. **First Rise:**
    - Place the dough in a lightly oiled bowl, cover with a cloth or plastic wrap, and let it rise in a warm, draft-free area for about 1-1.5 hours, or until doubled in size.

6. **Shape the Loaf:**
   - Punch down the dough and turn it out onto a floured surface.
   - Roll out the dough into a rectangle (about 12x16 inches).
   - Spread the poppy seed filling evenly over the dough.
   - Roll up the dough tightly from one long side to form a log.
   - Place the rolled dough seam-side down on a parchment-lined baking sheet or in a greased loaf pan.
7. **Second Rise:**
   - Cover and let the dough rise for another 30-45 minutes, or until puffy.
8. **Preheat the Oven:**
   - Preheat your oven to 375°F (190°C).
9. **Prepare for Baking:**
   - Brush the top of the loaf with the beaten egg and sprinkle with additional poppy seeds if desired.
10. **Bake:**
    - Bake for 35-40 minutes, or until the bread is golden brown and sounds hollow when tapped on the bottom.
11. **Cool:**
    - Allow the bread to cool on a wire rack before slicing.

Tips:

- **Filling Variations:** For a slightly different filling, you can add a bit of lemon zest or almond extract to the poppy seed mixture.
- **Texture:** If the dough is too sticky, add a bit more flour as needed.

Mohnbrot is perfect for breakfast, as a snack, or as part of a brunch spread. Its nutty, slightly sweet flavor and soft crumb make it a delicious choice for any meal. Enjoy your homemade poppy seed bread!

Kastenbrot

Ingredients:

- **For the Dough:**
    - 3 1/2 cups all-purpose flour
    - 1 1/2 cups warm milk (110°F or 45°C)
    - 1/4 cup sugar
    - 1/4 cup melted butter or vegetable oil
    - 2 teaspoons active dry yeast (or 1 packet)
    - 1 1/2 teaspoons salt
    - 1 large egg (optional, for added richness)

Instructions:

1. **Prepare the Yeast Mixture:**
    - In a small bowl, combine warm milk and sugar. Stir to dissolve.
    - Sprinkle the yeast over the mixture and let it sit for 5-10 minutes, until frothy.
2. **Mix the Dough:**
    - In a large bowl, combine flour and salt.
    - Add the yeast mixture, melted butter (or oil), and egg (if using). Mix until a dough forms.
3. **Knead the Dough:**
    - Turn the dough onto a floured surface and knead for about 8-10 minutes, until smooth and elastic.
4. **First Rise:**
    - Place the dough in a lightly oiled bowl, cover with a cloth or plastic wrap, and let it rise in a warm, draft-free area for about 1-1.5 hours, or until doubled in size.
5. **Shape the Loaf:**
    - Punch down the dough and turn it out onto a floured surface.
    - Shape the dough into a loaf and place it in a greased 9x5-inch loaf pan.
6. **Second Rise:**
    - Cover the pan with a cloth or plastic wrap and let the dough rise for another 30-45 minutes, or until puffy and nearly doubled.
7. **Preheat the Oven:**
    - Preheat your oven to 375°F (190°C).
8. **Bake:**
    - Bake for 30-35 minutes, or until the bread is golden brown and sounds hollow when tapped on the bottom.
9. **Cool:**
    - Allow the bread to cool in the pan for about 10 minutes, then transfer it to a wire rack to cool completely before slicing.

Tips:

- **Texture:** If you prefer a softer crust, cover the loaf with foil during the last 10 minutes of baking.
- **Flavor Variations:** You can add herbs, cheese, or seeds to the dough for added flavor. Simply fold them in during the kneading process.

Kastenbrot is a staple recipe for homemade bread and can be used in a variety of ways, from sandwiches to toast. Its simple preparation and delicious results make it a great addition to your baking repertoire. Enjoy your fresh, homemade loaf!

Brezenbrot

Ingredients:

- **For the Dough:**
    - 3 1/2 cups all-purpose flour
    - 1 1/2 cups warm water (110°F or 45°C)
    - 2 tablespoons sugar
    - 2 teaspoons active dry yeast (or 1 packet)
    - 1/4 cup unsalted butter, melted
    - 1 1/2 teaspoons salt
- **For the Baking Soda Bath:**
    - 1/4 cup baking soda
    - 2 cups water
- **For the Topping:**
    - Coarse sea salt (for sprinkling)
    - 1 egg, beaten (for egg wash)

Instructions:

1. **Prepare the Yeast Mixture:**
    - In a small bowl, combine warm water and sugar. Stir to dissolve.
    - Sprinkle the yeast over the mixture and let it sit for 5-10 minutes, until frothy.
2. **Mix the Dough:**
    - In a large bowl, combine flour and salt.
    - Add the yeast mixture and melted butter. Mix until a dough forms.
3. **Knead the Dough:**
    - Turn the dough onto a floured surface and knead for about 8-10 minutes, until smooth and elastic.
4. **First Rise:**
    - Place the dough in a lightly oiled bowl, cover with a cloth or plastic wrap, and let it rise in a warm, draft-free area for about 1-1.5 hours, or until doubled in size.
5. **Shape the Dough:**
    - Punch down the dough and turn it out onto a floured surface.
    - Shape the dough into a loaf and place it on a parchment-lined baking sheet.
6. **Prepare the Baking Soda Bath:**
    - In a large saucepan, bring 2 cups of water to a boil. Add the baking soda and stir until dissolved. Remove from heat.
7. **Dip the Dough:**
    - Carefully dip the shaped dough into the baking soda bath for about 30 seconds. Use a slotted spoon to remove it and place it back on the parchment-lined baking sheet.

8. **Second Rise:**
   - Let the dough rise for another 20-30 minutes, or until slightly puffy.
9. **Preheat the Oven:**
   - Preheat your oven to 375°F (190°C).
10. **Prepare for Baking:**
    - Brush the top of the loaf with the beaten egg and sprinkle with coarse sea salt.
11. **Bake:**
    - Bake for 30-35 minutes, or until the bread is golden brown and sounds hollow when tapped on the bottom.
12. **Cool:**
    - Allow the bread to cool on a wire rack before slicing.

Tips:

- **Crust:** For a crispier crust, bake the bread on a baking stone or an inverted baking sheet.
- **Flavor:** You can add caraway seeds or pretzel salt to the dough for extra flavor.

Brezenbrot is perfect for sandwiches, or simply enjoyed with a bit of butter or cheese. Its unique pretzel flavor and chewy texture make it a delightful bread to bake and enjoy.

Knäckebrot

Ingredients:

- **For the Dough:**
    - 2 cups whole wheat flour
    - 1 cup all-purpose flour
    - 1/2 cup rye flour (optional, for extra flavor)
    - 1 teaspoon salt
    - 1/2 teaspoon baking powder
    - 1/4 cup sunflower seeds (optional)
    - 1/4 cup sesame seeds (optional)
    - 1/2 cup water
    - 1/4 cup vegetable oil or melted butter
    - 1 tablespoon honey or sugar (optional, for a hint of sweetness)

Instructions:

1. **Preheat the Oven:**
    - Preheat your oven to 400°F (200°C). Line a baking sheet with parchment paper.
2. **Mix the Dough:**
    - In a large bowl, combine whole wheat flour, all-purpose flour, rye flour (if using), salt, and baking powder.
    - Stir in the sunflower and sesame seeds if using.
    - Add the water, vegetable oil (or melted butter), and honey (or sugar). Mix until a dough forms.
3. **Roll Out the Dough:**
    - Turn the dough onto a lightly floured surface and roll it out as thinly as possible, about 1/8 inch thick.
    - Transfer the rolled dough to the prepared baking sheet.
4. **Score the Dough:**
    - Use a knife or pizza cutter to score the dough into squares or rectangles. This makes it easier to break into pieces after baking.
5. **Bake:**
    - Bake in the preheated oven for 15-20 minutes, or until the crispbread is golden brown and crisp.
6. **Cool:**
    - Allow the crispbread to cool on a wire rack. Break into pieces along the scored lines.

Tips:

- **Texture:** For a crunchier texture, roll the dough thinner and bake a little longer if needed.
- **Flavor:** Experiment with adding different seeds, herbs, or spices to the dough for varied flavors.

Knäckebrot is versatile and can be topped with cheese, spreads, or enjoyed plain. Its crisp texture and simple ingredients make it a delightful addition to any meal. Enjoy your homemade crispbread!

Spelt Bread

Ingredients:

- **For the Dough:**
    - 3 1/2 cups spelt flour
    - 1 1/2 cups warm water (110°F or 45°C)
    - 2 tablespoons honey or maple syrup
    - 2 teaspoons active dry yeast (or 1 packet)
    - 1 1/2 teaspoons salt
    - 1/4 cup olive oil or melted butter
    - 1 egg (optional, for added richness)

Instructions:

1. **Prepare the Yeast Mixture:**
    - In a small bowl, combine warm water and honey (or maple syrup). Stir to dissolve.
    - Sprinkle the yeast over the mixture and let it sit for 5-10 minutes, until frothy.
2. **Mix the Dough:**
    - In a large bowl, combine spelt flour and salt.
    - Add the yeast mixture, olive oil (or melted butter), and egg (if using). Mix until a dough forms.
3. **Knead the Dough:**
    - Turn the dough onto a floured surface and knead for about 8-10 minutes, until smooth and elastic.
4. **First Rise:**
    - Place the dough in a lightly oiled bowl, cover with a cloth or plastic wrap, and let it rise in a warm, draft-free area for about 1-1.5 hours, or until doubled in size.
5. **Shape the Loaf:**
    - Punch down the dough and turn it out onto a floured surface.
    - Shape the dough into a loaf and place it in a greased 9x5-inch loaf pan.
6. **Second Rise:**
    - Cover the pan with a cloth or plastic wrap and let the dough rise for another 30-45 minutes, or until puffy and nearly doubled.
7. **Preheat the Oven:**
    - Preheat your oven to 375°F (190°C).
8. **Bake:**
    - Bake for 30-35 minutes, or until the bread is golden brown and sounds hollow when tapped on the bottom.
9. **Cool:**

- Allow the bread to cool in the pan for about 10 minutes, then transfer it to a wire rack to cool completely before slicing.

Tips:

- **Texture:** Spelt flour has less gluten than wheat, so the bread may be denser. Ensure proper kneading and rising for best results.
- **Flavor Variations:** Add herbs, seeds, or nuts to the dough for extra flavor.

Spelt Bread is a hearty and nutritious choice, great for sandwiches, toast, or as an accompaniment to soups and salads. Enjoy your homemade spelt bread!

Kümmelbrot

Ingredients:

- **For the Dough:**
    - 3 1/2 cups all-purpose flour
    - 1 1/2 cups warm water (110°F or 45°C)
    - 2 tablespoons sugar or honey
    - 2 teaspoons active dry yeast (or 1 packet)
    - 1 1/2 teaspoons salt
    - 2 tablespoons caraway seeds
    - 1/4 cup vegetable oil or melted butter
- **For the Topping (optional):**
    - Additional caraway seeds
    - 1 egg, beaten (for egg wash)

Instructions:

1. **Prepare the Yeast Mixture:**
    - In a small bowl, combine warm water and sugar (or honey). Stir to dissolve.
    - Sprinkle the yeast over the mixture and let it sit for 5-10 minutes, until frothy.
2. **Mix the Dough:**
    - In a large bowl, combine flour, salt, and caraway seeds.
    - Add the yeast mixture and vegetable oil (or melted butter). Mix until a dough forms.
3. **Knead the Dough:**
    - Turn the dough onto a floured surface and knead for about 8-10 minutes, until smooth and elastic.
4. **First Rise:**
    - Place the dough in a lightly oiled bowl, cover with a cloth or plastic wrap, and let it rise in a warm, draft-free area for about 1-1.5 hours, or until doubled in size.
5. **Shape the Loaf:**
    - Punch down the dough and turn it out onto a floured surface.
    - Shape the dough into a loaf or divide into smaller loaves. Place on a parchment-lined baking sheet or in greased loaf pans.
6. **Second Rise:**
    - Cover and let the dough rise for another 30-45 minutes, or until puffy.
7. **Preheat the Oven:**
    - Preheat your oven to 375°F (190°C).
8. **Prepare for Baking:**
    - Brush the top of the loaf with the beaten egg if using and sprinkle additional caraway seeds on top.

9. **Bake:**
   - Bake for 30-35 minutes, or until the bread is golden brown and sounds hollow when tapped on the bottom.
10. **Cool:**
    - Allow the bread to cool on a wire rack before slicing.

Tips:

- **Texture:** For a slightly different texture, you can use a mix of whole wheat and all-purpose flour.
- **Flavor:** If you want a more intense caraway flavor, increase the amount of seeds.

Kümmelbrot's aromatic flavor and hearty texture make it a delicious choice for various meals. It's especially good with hearty soups or as a base for savory spreads and cheeses. Enjoy baking and savoring your homemade caraway bread!

Bauernlandbrot

Ingredients:

- **For the Dough:**
    - 2 1/2 cups all-purpose flour
    - 1 1/2 cups rye flour
    - 1 1/2 cups warm water (110°F or 45°C)
    - 2 teaspoons active dry yeast (or 1 packet)
    - 2 tablespoons sugar or honey
    - 2 teaspoons salt
    - 1/4 cup sourdough starter (optional, for added flavor)
    - 1/4 cup vegetable oil or melted butter

Instructions:

1. **Prepare the Yeast Mixture:**
    - In a small bowl, combine warm water and sugar (or honey). Stir to dissolve.
    - Sprinkle the yeast over the mixture and let it sit for 5-10 minutes, until frothy.
2. **Mix the Dough:**
    - In a large bowl, combine all-purpose flour, rye flour, and salt.
    - Add the yeast mixture, sourdough starter (if using), and vegetable oil (or melted butter). Mix until a dough forms.
3. **Knead the Dough:**
    - Turn the dough onto a floured surface and knead for about 8-10 minutes, until smooth and elastic.
4. **First Rise:**
    - Place the dough in a lightly oiled bowl, cover with a cloth or plastic wrap, and let it rise in a warm, draft-free area for about 1-1.5 hours, or until doubled in size.
5. **Shape the Loaf:**
    - Punch down the dough and turn it out onto a floured surface.
    - Shape the dough into a round or oval loaf and place it on a parchment-lined baking sheet or in a greased Dutch oven or loaf pan.
6. **Second Rise:**
    - Cover and let the dough rise for another 30-45 minutes, or until puffy.
7. **Preheat the Oven:**
    - Preheat your oven to 375°F (190°C).
8. **Bake:**
    - Bake for 35-45 minutes, or until the bread is golden brown and sounds hollow when tapped on the bottom.
9. **Cool:**
    - Allow the bread to cool on a wire rack before slicing.

Tips:

- **Crust:** For a crispier crust, bake the bread in a Dutch oven with the lid on for the first 20 minutes, then remove the lid for the remaining baking time.
- **Flavor:** If you like, you can add caraway seeds or sunflower seeds to the dough for extra flavor and texture.

Bauernlandbrot is a hearty, versatile bread with a rustic appeal, making it a wonderful addition to any meal. Enjoy it fresh from the oven or toasted with your favorite toppings!

Knoblauchbrot

Ingredients:

- **For the Bread:**
  - 1 loaf of Italian or French bread (or a similar crusty bread)
- **For the Garlic Butter Spread:**
  - 1/2 cup unsalted butter, softened
  - 4-6 cloves garlic, minced (adjust to taste)
  - 1/4 cup fresh parsley, chopped (or 2 tablespoons dried parsley)
  - 1/4 teaspoon salt
  - 1/4 teaspoon black pepper
  - 1/4 teaspoon crushed red pepper flakes (optional, for a bit of heat)

Instructions:

1. **Prepare the Garlic Butter:**
   - In a bowl, combine the softened butter, minced garlic, chopped parsley, salt, pepper, and red pepper flakes (if using). Mix until well combined.
2. **Prepare the Bread:**
   - Preheat your oven to 375°F (190°C).
   - Slice the loaf of bread in half lengthwise, or into individual slices if you prefer smaller pieces.
3. **Spread the Butter:**
   - Evenly spread the garlic butter mixture over the cut sides of the bread.
4. **Bake:**
   - Place the bread halves on a baking sheet, cut side up.
   - Bake for 10-15 minutes, or until the edges are golden and the butter is melted. For a crispier top, broil for an additional 1-2 minutes, but watch closely to avoid burning.
5. **Serve:**
   - Remove from the oven and let cool slightly before slicing if you haven't already.

Tips:

- **Fresh Garlic:** For a milder garlic flavor, you can roast the garlic before adding it to the butter.
- **Cheesy Variation:** Add grated Parmesan or shredded mozzarella to the garlic butter for a cheesy twist.

Knoblauchbrot is a crowd-pleaser and a versatile addition to many meals. Enjoy the rich, savory flavor of homemade garlic bread!

Hefezopf

Ingredients:

- **For the Dough:**
    - 4 cups all-purpose flour
    - 1/2 cup sugar
    - 1 cup warm milk (110°F or 45°C)
    - 1/4 cup unsalted butter, melted
    - 2 large eggs
    - 2 teaspoons active dry yeast (or 1 packet)
    - 1/2 teaspoon salt
    - 1/2 teaspoon ground cardamom (optional, for a traditional touch)
- **For the Egg Wash:**
    - 1 egg, beaten
    - 1 tablespoon milk
- **For the Topping (optional):**
    - Sliced almonds
    - Sugar

Instructions:

1. **Prepare the Yeast Mixture:**
    - In a small bowl, combine warm milk and 1 tablespoon sugar. Stir to dissolve.
    - Sprinkle the yeast over the mixture and let it sit for 5-10 minutes, until frothy.
2. **Mix the Dough:**
    - In a large bowl, combine flour, remaining sugar, salt, and cardamom (if using).
    - Add the yeast mixture, melted butter, and eggs. Mix until a dough forms.
3. **Knead the Dough:**
    - Turn the dough onto a floured surface and knead for about 8-10 minutes, until smooth and elastic.
4. **First Rise:**
    - Place the dough in a lightly oiled bowl, cover with a cloth or plastic wrap, and let it rise in a warm, draft-free area for about 1-1.5 hours, or until doubled in size.
5. **Shape the Dough:**
    - Punch down the dough and turn it out onto a floured surface.
    - Divide the dough into three equal portions. Roll each portion into a long strip, about 18 inches long.
    - Braid the three strips together and pinch the ends to seal. Place the braided dough on a parchment-lined baking sheet.
6. **Second Rise:**

- Cover the braided dough with a cloth and let it rise for another 30-45 minutes, or until puffy.
7. **Preheat the Oven:**
    - Preheat your oven to 375°F (190°C).
8. **Prepare for Baking:**
    - Brush the top of the dough with the beaten egg mixed with milk. Sprinkle with sliced almonds and sugar if desired.
9. **Bake:**
    - Bake for 25-30 minutes, or until golden brown and cooked through.
10. **Cool:**
    - Allow the Hefezopf to cool on a wire rack before slicing.

Tips:

- **Texture:** For a softer crust, cover the bread with foil for the last 10 minutes of baking.
- **Flavor:** You can add raisins or dried fruit to the dough for extra sweetness.

Hefezopf is perfect for breakfast, brunch, or as a sweet snack. Enjoy the soft, sweet bread with your favorite spread or on its own!

Poppy Seed Bread

Ingredients:

- **For the Dough:**
    - 3 1/2 cups all-purpose flour
    - 1 cup warm milk (110°F or 45°C)
    - 1/2 cup sugar
    - 1/4 cup unsalted butter, softened
    - 2 large eggs
    - 2 teaspoons active dry yeast (or 1 packet)
    - 1/4 cup poppy seeds
    - 1/2 teaspoon salt
- **For the Glaze (optional):**
    - 1/4 cup powdered sugar
    - 2 tablespoons milk
    - 1/2 teaspoon vanilla extract

Instructions:

1. **Prepare the Yeast Mixture:**
    - In a small bowl, combine warm milk and 1 tablespoon of sugar. Stir to dissolve.
    - Sprinkle the yeast over the mixture and let it sit for 5-10 minutes, until frothy.
2. **Mix the Dough:**
    - In a large bowl, combine flour, remaining sugar, and salt.
    - Add the yeast mixture, softened butter, and eggs. Mix until a dough forms.
3. **Knead the Dough:**
    - Turn the dough onto a floured surface and knead for about 8-10 minutes, until smooth and elastic.
    - Incorporate the poppy seeds during the last few minutes of kneading.
4. **First Rise:**
    - Place the dough in a lightly oiled bowl, cover with a cloth or plastic wrap, and let it rise in a warm, draft-free area for about 1-1.5 hours, or until doubled in size.
5. **Shape the Loaf:**
    - Punch down the dough and turn it out onto a floured surface.
    - Shape the dough into a loaf and place it in a greased 9x5-inch loaf pan.
6. **Second Rise:**
    - Cover the pan with a cloth and let the dough rise for another 30-45 minutes, or until puffy.
7. **Preheat the Oven:**
    - Preheat your oven to 375°F (190°C).
8. **Bake:**

- Bake for 30-35 minutes, or until the bread is golden brown and sounds hollow when tapped on the bottom.
9. **Prepare the Glaze (optional):**
    - While the bread cools, mix powdered sugar, milk, and vanilla extract in a small bowl. Drizzle over the cooled bread.
10. **Cool:**
    - Allow the bread to cool in the pan for 10 minutes, then transfer it to a wire rack to cool completely before slicing.

Tips:

- **Texture:** For a softer crust, you can cover the bread with foil during the last 10 minutes of baking.
- **Flavor Variation:** Add a tablespoon of lemon zest to the dough for a citrusy twist.

Poppy Seed Bread is delightful on its own or with a spread of butter, and its nutty flavor makes it a favorite for many. Enjoy your homemade bread!

Butterbrot

Ingredients:

- **For the Bread:**
    - 1 loaf of your favorite bread (such as German rye, sourdough, or a crusty baguette)
- **For the Butter:**
    - 1/2 cup unsalted butter, softened
    - A pinch of salt (if using unsalted butter)
    - Optional: Fresh herbs (like chives or parsley), freshly ground black pepper, or a sprinkle of sea salt

Instructions:

1. **Prepare the Bread:**
    - Slice the bread into individual pieces or serve the whole loaf if preferred. The bread should be fresh and crusty.
2. **Prepare the Butter:**
    - In a bowl, mix the softened butter with a pinch of salt if using unsalted butter. If you like, you can also mix in fresh herbs, pepper, or a bit of sea salt for extra flavor.
3. **Spread the Butter:**
    - Spread a generous layer of the butter mixture evenly over each slice of bread.
4. **Serve:**
    - Butterbrot can be served as a simple snack, an accompaniment to soups, or as part of a larger meal.

Tips:

- **Bread Choice:** Use a good-quality, fresh bread for the best flavor. A hearty rye or a crusty baguette works well.
- **Customization:** Add sliced radishes, cucumber, or a sprinkle of cheese on top of the butter for added variety.

Butterbrot is a perfect example of how simple ingredients can create a satisfying and comforting snack. Enjoy this classic German treat!

Studentenbrot

Ingredients:

- **For the Dough:**
    - 3 1/2 cups all-purpose flour
    - 1 1/2 cups whole wheat flour
    - 1 1/2 cups warm water (110°F or 45°C)
    - 2 teaspoons active dry yeast (or 1 packet)
    - 1/2 cup honey or molasses
    - 1/4 cup vegetable oil
    - 1 teaspoon salt
    - 1 cup mixed nuts (such as walnuts, almonds, or hazelnuts), chopped
    - 1/2 cup mixed dried fruits (such as raisins, cranberries, or apricots), chopped
    - 1/4 cup sunflower seeds or pumpkin seeds (optional)

Instructions:

1. **Prepare the Yeast Mixture:**
    - In a small bowl, combine warm water and honey (or molasses). Stir to dissolve.
    - Sprinkle the yeast over the mixture and let it sit for 5-10 minutes, until frothy.
2. **Mix the Dough:**
    - In a large bowl, combine all-purpose flour, whole wheat flour, and salt.
    - Add the yeast mixture, vegetable oil, nuts, dried fruits, and seeds. Mix until a dough forms.
3. **Knead the Dough:**
    - Turn the dough onto a floured surface and knead for about 8-10 minutes, until smooth and elastic.
4. **First Rise:**
    - Place the dough in a lightly oiled bowl, cover with a cloth or plastic wrap, and let it rise in a warm, draft-free area for about 1-1.5 hours, or until doubled in size.
5. **Shape the Loaf:**
    - Punch down the dough and turn it out onto a floured surface.
    - Shape the dough into a round or oval loaf and place it on a parchment-lined baking sheet or in a greased loaf pan.
6. **Second Rise:**
    - Cover the loaf with a cloth and let it rise for another 30-45 minutes, or until puffy.
7. **Preheat the Oven:**
    - Preheat your oven to 375°F (190°C).
8. **Bake:**
    - Bake for 35-45 minutes, or until the bread is golden brown and sounds hollow when tapped on the bottom.

9. **Cool:**
   - Allow the bread to cool on a wire rack before slicing.

Tips:

- **Texture:** For a crunchier crust, bake the bread in a Dutch oven with the lid on for the first 20 minutes, then remove the lid for the remaining baking time.
- **Flavor Variations:** Experiment with different nuts, seeds, and dried fruits to suit your taste.

Studentenbrot is nutritious and filling, making it a great choice for breakfast, snacks, or as part of a meal. Enjoy your homemade hearty bread!

Heidelbeerbrot

Ingredients:

- **For the Dough:**
    - 2 1/2 cups all-purpose flour
    - 1/2 cup sugar
    - 2 teaspoons baking powder
    - 1/2 teaspoon salt
    - 1/2 cup unsalted butter, softened
    - 2 large eggs
    - 1 cup milk
    - 1 cup fresh or frozen blueberries (do not thaw if frozen)
- **For the Topping (optional):**
    - 1 tablespoon sugar
    - 1/2 teaspoon cinnamon

Instructions:

1. **Preheat the Oven:**
    - Preheat your oven to 350°F (175°C).
    - Grease and flour a 9x5-inch loaf pan or line it with parchment paper.
2. **Mix Dry Ingredients:**
    - In a medium bowl, whisk together flour, sugar, baking powder, and salt.
3. **Cream Butter and Eggs:**
    - In a large bowl, beat the softened butter until creamy.
    - Add the eggs one at a time, beating well after each addition.
4. **Combine Ingredients:**
    - Gradually add the dry ingredients to the butter mixture, alternating with the milk. Mix until just combined.
    - Gently fold in the blueberries.
5. **Transfer to Pan:**
    - Pour the batter into the prepared loaf pan.
6. **Prepare Topping (optional):**
    - Mix sugar and cinnamon, then sprinkle over the top of the batter for added sweetness and texture.
7. **Bake:**
    - Bake for 50-60 minutes, or until a toothpick inserted into the center comes out clean.
8. **Cool:**
    - Allow the bread to cool in the pan for 10 minutes, then transfer to a wire rack to cool completely before slicing.

Tips:

- **Blueberry Handling:** Tossing the blueberries in a bit of flour before adding them to the batter can help prevent them from sinking.
- **Flavor Boost:** For added flavor, consider adding a teaspoon of lemon zest to the batter.

Heidelbeerbrot is a delightful and fruity bread that's perfect for enjoying with a cup of tea or coffee. Enjoy your homemade blueberry bread!

Kaffeebrot

Ingredients:

- **For the Dough:**
    - 3 1/2 cups all-purpose flour
    - 1/2 cup sugar
    - 1 cup warm milk (110°F or 45°C)
    - 1/4 cup unsalted butter, softened
    - 2 large eggs
    - 2 teaspoons active dry yeast (or 1 packet)
    - 1/2 teaspoon salt
    - 1/2 teaspoon ground cinnamon (optional)
    - 1/2 cup chopped nuts (like walnuts or almonds) or dried fruit (like raisins or currants) (optional)
- **For the Glaze (optional):**
    - 1/4 cup powdered sugar
    - 2 tablespoons milk
    - 1/2 teaspoon vanilla extract

Instructions:

1. **Prepare the Yeast Mixture:**
    - In a small bowl, combine warm milk and 1 tablespoon sugar. Stir to dissolve.
    - Sprinkle the yeast over the mixture and let it sit for 5-10 minutes, until frothy.
2. **Mix the Dough:**
    - In a large bowl, combine flour, remaining sugar, salt, and cinnamon (if using).
    - Add the yeast mixture, softened butter, and eggs. Mix until a dough forms.
    - If using, fold in the nuts or dried fruit.
3. **Knead the Dough:**
    - Turn the dough onto a floured surface and knead for about 8-10 minutes, until smooth and elastic.
4. **First Rise:**
    - Place the dough in a lightly oiled bowl, cover with a cloth or plastic wrap, and let it rise in a warm, draft-free area for about 1-1.5 hours, or until doubled in size.
5. **Shape the Loaf:**
    - Punch down the dough and turn it out onto a floured surface.
    - Shape the dough into a loaf and place it in a greased 9x5-inch loaf pan or on a parchment-lined baking sheet.
6. **Second Rise:**
    - Cover the loaf and let it rise for another 30-45 minutes, or until puffy.
7. **Preheat the Oven:**

- Preheat your oven to 375°F (190°C).
8. **Bake:**
    - Bake for 30-35 minutes, or until the bread is golden brown and sounds hollow when tapped on the bottom.
9. **Prepare the Glaze (optional):**
    - Mix powdered sugar, milk, and vanilla extract in a small bowl. Drizzle over the cooled bread.
10. **Cool:**
    - Allow the bread to cool in the pan for 10 minutes, then transfer to a wire rack to cool completely before slicing.

Tips:

- **Flavor Variations:** You can add spices like nutmeg or cardamom for extra flavor, or incorporate a bit of lemon zest.
- **Texture:** For a softer crust, cover the bread with foil during the last 10 minutes of baking.

Kaffeebrot is a versatile and enjoyable bread, perfect for a cozy coffee break or as a sweet treat any time of day. Enjoy!

Walnussbrot

Ingredients:

- **For the Dough:**
    - 3 1/2 cups all-purpose flour
    - 1/2 cup whole wheat flour (optional, for added texture and flavor)
    - 1 1/2 cups warm water (110°F or 45°C)
    - 2 teaspoons active dry yeast (or 1 packet)
    - 1/4 cup honey or sugar
    - 1/4 cup olive oil or unsalted butter, melted
    - 1 teaspoon salt
    - 1 1/2 cups chopped walnuts (toasted if desired)

Instructions:

1. **Prepare the Yeast Mixture:**
    - In a small bowl, combine warm water and honey (or sugar). Stir to dissolve.
    - Sprinkle the yeast over the mixture and let it sit for 5-10 minutes, until frothy.
2. **Mix the Dough:**
    - In a large bowl, combine all-purpose flour, whole wheat flour (if using), and salt.
    - Add the yeast mixture, olive oil (or melted butter), and mix until a dough forms.
    - Gently fold in the chopped walnuts.
3. **Knead the Dough:**
    - Turn the dough onto a floured surface and knead for about 8-10 minutes, until smooth and elastic.
4. **First Rise:**
    - Place the dough in a lightly oiled bowl, cover with a cloth or plastic wrap, and let it rise in a warm, draft-free area for about 1-1.5 hours, or until doubled in size.
5. **Shape the Loaf:**
    - Punch down the dough and turn it out onto a floured surface.
    - Shape the dough into a loaf and place it in a greased 9x5-inch loaf pan or on a parchment-lined baking sheet.
6. **Second Rise:**
    - Cover the loaf and let it rise for another 30-45 minutes, or until puffy.
7. **Preheat the Oven:**
    - Preheat your oven to 375°F (190°C).
8. **Bake:**
    - Bake for 30-35 minutes, or until the bread is golden brown and sounds hollow when tapped on the bottom.
9. **Cool:**

- Allow the bread to cool in the pan for 10 minutes, then transfer to a wire rack to cool completely before slicing.

Tips:

- **Toasting Walnuts:** Toasting walnuts can enhance their flavor. Simply spread them on a baking sheet and toast in a 350°F (175°C) oven for about 8-10 minutes, stirring occasionally.
- **Variations:** For added flavor, you can mix in some dried fruit like cranberries or raisins.

Walnussbrot has a wonderful nutty aroma and a satisfying texture, making it a great addition to any meal or a delicious standalone treat. Enjoy your homemade walnut bread!

Roggen-Karotten-Brot

Ingredients:

- **For the Dough:**
    - 2 cups rye flour
    - 1 1/2 cups all-purpose flour
    - 1 cup grated carrots (about 2 medium carrots)
    - 1 1/2 cups warm water (110°F or 45°C)
    - 2 teaspoons active dry yeast (or 1 packet)
    - 2 tablespoons honey or sugar
    - 1/4 cup olive oil or unsalted butter, melted
    - 1 teaspoon salt
    - 1/2 teaspoon ground caraway seeds (optional, for traditional flavor)

Instructions:

1. **Prepare the Yeast Mixture:**
    - In a small bowl, combine warm water and honey (or sugar). Stir to dissolve.
    - Sprinkle the yeast over the mixture and let it sit for 5-10 minutes, until frothy.
2. **Mix the Dough:**
    - In a large bowl, combine rye flour, all-purpose flour, and salt. Add caraway seeds if using.
    - Add the yeast mixture, olive oil (or melted butter), and grated carrots. Mix until a dough forms.
3. **Knead the Dough:**
    - Turn the dough onto a floured surface and knead for about 8-10 minutes, until smooth and elastic.
4. **First Rise:**
    - Place the dough in a lightly oiled bowl, cover with a cloth or plastic wrap, and let it rise in a warm, draft-free area for about 1-1.5 hours, or until doubled in size.
5. **Shape the Loaf:**
    - Punch down the dough and turn it out onto a floured surface.
    - Shape the dough into a loaf and place it in a greased 9x5-inch loaf pan or on a parchment-lined baking sheet.
6. **Second Rise:**
    - Cover the loaf and let it rise for another 30-45 minutes, or until puffy.
7. **Preheat the Oven:**
    - Preheat your oven to 375°F (190°C).
8. **Bake:**
    - Bake for 35-45 minutes, or until the bread is golden brown and sounds hollow when tapped on the bottom.

9. **Cool:**
    - Allow the bread to cool in the pan for 10 minutes, then transfer to a wire rack to cool completely before slicing.

Tips:

- **Carrots:** Grate the carrots finely to ensure they integrate well into the dough and don't make the bread too dense.
- **Texture:** For a slightly denser bread, you can use all rye flour, but it might be a bit heavier.

Roggen-Karotten-Brot combines the wholesome taste of rye with the subtle sweetness of carrots, making it a unique and tasty bread option. Enjoy!

Baguette Brot

Ingredients:

- **For the Dough:**
    - 3 1/2 cups all-purpose flour (plus extra for dusting)
    - 1 1/2 cups warm water (110°F or 45°C)
    - 2 teaspoons active dry yeast (or 1 packet)
    - 1 1/2 teaspoons salt
    - 1 tablespoon sugar (optional, to help the yeast)
- **For the Glaze (optional):**
    - 1/4 cup water
    - 1 tablespoon all-purpose flour

Instructions:

1. **Prepare the Yeast Mixture:**
    - In a small bowl, combine warm water and sugar (if using). Stir to dissolve.
    - Sprinkle the yeast over the mixture and let it sit for 5-10 minutes, until frothy.
2. **Mix the Dough:**
    - In a large bowl, combine flour and salt.
    - Add the yeast mixture to the flour mixture and stir until a dough forms.
3. **Knead the Dough:**
    - Turn the dough onto a floured surface and knead for about 8-10 minutes, until smooth and elastic.
4. **First Rise:**
    - Place the dough in a lightly oiled bowl, cover with a cloth or plastic wrap, and let it rise in a warm, draft-free area for about 1-1.5 hours, or until doubled in size.
5. **Preheat the Oven:**
    - Preheat your oven to 475°F (245°C). Place a baking stone or an inverted baking sheet in the oven to heat.
6. **Shape the Baguettes:**
    - Punch down the dough and turn it out onto a floured surface.
    - Divide the dough into 2-3 equal pieces.
    - Gently shape each piece into a long, thin loaf (about 16-18 inches long) with tapered ends.
7. **Second Rise:**
    - Place the shaped baguettes on a floured baguette pan or a parchment-lined baking sheet.
    - Cover with a cloth and let rise for 30-45 minutes, or until puffy.
8. **Prepare for Baking:**

- 9. **Bake:**
    - Make a few shallow slashes diagonally across the top of each baguette with a sharp knife or a razor blade.
    - Place the baguettes in the preheated oven. For a crispier crust, place a pan of hot water on the lower rack of the oven to create steam.
    - Bake for 20-25 minutes, or until the baguettes are golden brown and sound hollow when tapped on the bottom.
- 10. **Cool:**
    - Transfer the baked baguettes to a wire rack to cool completely before slicing.

Tips:

- **Steam:** Creating steam in the oven helps achieve the classic crispy crust. You can use a spray bottle to mist the baguettes with water just before baking.
- **Shaping:** Be gentle when shaping the baguettes to avoid deflating the dough too much.

Baguette Brot is a delightful bread that's perfect for sandwiches, dipping into soups, or enjoying with cheese. Enjoy the process and the delicious results!

Schrotbrot

Ingredients:

- **For the Dough:**
    - 2 cups rye flour
    - 1 cup whole wheat flour
    - 1 cup coarsely ground rye or wheat grits (also known as meal or cracked grains)
    - 1 1/2 cups warm water (110°F or 45°C)
    - 2 teaspoons active dry yeast (or 1 packet)
    - 1 tablespoon honey or sugar
    - 1/4 cup vegetable oil or melted butter
    - 1 teaspoon salt
    - 1/2 teaspoon caraway seeds (optional)

Instructions:

1. **Prepare the Yeast Mixture:**
    - In a small bowl, combine warm water and honey (or sugar). Stir to dissolve.
    - Sprinkle the yeast over the mixture and let it sit for 5-10 minutes, until frothy.
2. **Mix the Dough:**
    - In a large bowl, combine rye flour, whole wheat flour, coarsely ground grits, and salt. Add caraway seeds if using.
    - Add the yeast mixture and oil (or melted butter). Mix until a dough forms.
3. **Knead the Dough:**
    - Turn the dough onto a floured surface and knead for about 8-10 minutes, until smooth and elastic.
4. **First Rise:**
    - Place the dough in a lightly oiled bowl, cover with a cloth or plastic wrap, and let it rise in a warm, draft-free area for about 1-1.5 hours, or until doubled in size.
5. **Shape the Loaf:**
    - Punch down the dough and turn it out onto a floured surface.
    - Shape the dough into a round or oval loaf and place it in a greased 9x5-inch loaf pan or on a parchment-lined baking sheet.
6. **Second Rise:**
    - Cover the loaf and let it rise for another 30-45 minutes, or until puffy.
7. **Preheat the Oven:**
    - Preheat your oven to 375°F (190°C).
8. **Bake:**
    - Bake for 35-45 minutes, or until the bread is golden brown and sounds hollow when tapped on the bottom.
9. **Cool:**

- Allow the bread to cool in the pan for 10 minutes, then transfer to a wire rack to cool completely before slicing.

Tips:

- **Texture:** The coarsely ground grains contribute to the hearty texture of Schrotbrot. If you prefer a finer texture, you can grind the grains a bit more.
- **Flavor Variations:** Add seeds like sunflower or pumpkin for extra flavor and crunch.

Schrotbrot is perfect for sandwiches or enjoyed with butter and cheese. Its robust flavor and satisfying texture make it a great staple for any bread lover. Enjoy!

Roggen-Mehrkornbrot

Ingredients:

- **For the Dough:**
    - 2 cups rye flour
    - 1 cup whole wheat flour
    - 1 cup all-purpose flour
    - 1/2 cup rolled oats
    - 1/4 cup sunflower seeds
    - 1/4 cup pumpkin seeds
    - 1/4 cup flaxseeds
    - 2 tablespoons sesame seeds
    - 1 1/2 cups warm water (110°F or 45°C)
    - 2 teaspoons active dry yeast (or 1 packet)
    - 2 tablespoons honey or molasses
    - 1/4 cup vegetable oil or melted butter
    - 1 teaspoon salt

Instructions:

1. **Prepare the Yeast Mixture:**
    - In a small bowl, combine warm water and honey (or molasses). Stir to dissolve.
    - Sprinkle the yeast over the mixture and let it sit for 5-10 minutes, until frothy.
2. **Mix the Dough:**
    - In a large bowl, combine rye flour, whole wheat flour, all-purpose flour, salt, and all the seeds and oats.
    - Add the yeast mixture and oil (or melted butter). Mix until a dough forms.
3. **Knead the Dough:**
    - Turn the dough onto a floured surface and knead for about 8-10 minutes, until smooth and elastic.
4. **First Rise:**
    - Place the dough in a lightly oiled bowl, cover with a cloth or plastic wrap, and let it rise in a warm, draft-free area for about 1-1.5 hours, or until doubled in size.
5. **Shape the Loaf:**
    - Punch down the dough and turn it out onto a floured surface.
    - Shape the dough into a loaf and place it in a greased 9x5-inch loaf pan or on a parchment-lined baking sheet.
6. **Second Rise:**
    - Cover the loaf and let it rise for another 30-45 minutes, or until puffy.
7. **Preheat the Oven:**
    - Preheat your oven to 375°F (190°C).

8. **Bake:**
    - Bake for 35-45 minutes, or until the bread is golden brown and sounds hollow when tapped on the bottom.
9. **Cool:**
    - Allow the bread to cool in the pan for 10 minutes, then transfer to a wire rack to cool completely before slicing.

Tips:

- **Seed Variations:** Feel free to experiment with different seeds or nuts according to your preference.
- **Texture:** For an even heartier bread, you can add additional grains like quinoa or barley.

Roggen-Mehrkornbrot is a robust and satisfying bread that's perfect for sandwiches or as a side with soups and salads. Enjoy the rich, nutty flavors!

Keksbrot

Ingredients:

- **For the Dough:**
    - 2 1/2 cups all-purpose flour
    - 1/2 cup sugar
    - 1/2 teaspoon salt
    - 1/2 cup unsalted butter, softened
    - 2 large eggs
    - 1 cup milk
    - 1 tablespoon baking powder
    - 1 teaspoon vanilla extract
    - 1/2 cup chocolate chips or dried fruit (optional)
    - 1/2 teaspoon ground cinnamon (optional)
- **For the Topping (optional):**
    - 2 tablespoons sugar
    - 1/2 teaspoon ground cinnamon

Instructions:

1. **Preheat the Oven:**
    - Preheat your oven to 350°F (175°C).
    - Grease and flour a 9x5-inch loaf pan or line it with parchment paper.
2. **Mix Dry Ingredients:**
    - In a medium bowl, whisk together flour, sugar, salt, and baking powder. If using cinnamon, add it to the mixture.
3. **Cream Butter and Eggs:**
    - In a large bowl, beat the softened butter until creamy.
    - Add the eggs one at a time, beating well after each addition.
    - Stir in the vanilla extract.
4. **Combine Ingredients:**
    - Gradually add the dry ingredients to the butter mixture, alternating with the milk. Mix until just combined.
    - Fold in chocolate chips or dried fruit if using.
5. **Transfer to Pan:**
    - Pour the batter into the prepared loaf pan.
6. **Prepare Topping (optional):**
    - Mix sugar and cinnamon in a small bowl.
    - Sprinkle over the top of the batter for added sweetness and a touch of spice.
7. **Bake:**

- Bake for 50-60 minutes, or until a toothpick inserted into the center comes out clean.
8. **Cool:**
    - Allow the bread to cool in the pan for 10 minutes, then transfer to a wire rack to cool completely before slicing.

Tips:

- **Texture:** Keksbrot is typically a bit denser than traditional bread due to the addition of sugar and butter.
- **Add-Ins:** You can customize this bread by adding nuts, seeds, or even a swirl of jam for extra flavor.

Keksbrot is a sweet treat that combines the best aspects of cookies and bread, making it a delightful addition to your baking repertoire. Enjoy your homemade Keksbrot!

Pfefferminzbrot

Ingredients:

- **For the Dough:**
    - 3 1/2 cups all-purpose flour
    - 1 1/2 cups warm water (110°F or 45°C)
    - 2 teaspoons active dry yeast (or 1 packet)
    - 1 tablespoon sugar
    - 1/4 cup olive oil or melted butter
    - 1 teaspoon salt
    - 1/4 cup fresh mint leaves, finely chopped (or 2 tablespoons dried mint)
    - 1 tablespoon chopped fresh rosemary (optional)
- **For the Glaze (optional):**
    - 1 tablespoon milk
    - 1 tablespoon sugar

Instructions:

1. **Prepare the Yeast Mixture:**
    - In a small bowl, combine warm water and sugar. Stir to dissolve.
    - Sprinkle the yeast over the mixture and let it sit for 5-10 minutes, until frothy.
2. **Mix the Dough:**
    - In a large bowl, combine flour and salt.
    - Add the yeast mixture and olive oil (or melted butter) to the flour. Mix until a dough forms.
    - Fold in the chopped mint leaves and rosemary if using.
3. **Knead the Dough:**
    - Turn the dough onto a floured surface and knead for about 8-10 minutes, until smooth and elastic.
4. **First Rise:**
    - Place the dough in a lightly oiled bowl, cover with a cloth or plastic wrap, and let it rise in a warm, draft-free area for about 1-1.5 hours, or until doubled in size.
5. **Shape the Loaf:**
    - Punch down the dough and turn it out onto a floured surface.
    - Shape the dough into a loaf and place it in a greased 9x5-inch loaf pan or on a parchment-lined baking sheet.
6. **Second Rise:**
    - Cover the loaf and let it rise for another 30-45 minutes, or until puffy.
7. **Preheat the Oven:**
    - Preheat your oven to 375°F (190°C).
8. **Prepare the Glaze (optional):**

- Mix milk and sugar in a small bowl.
- Brush the mixture over the top of the loaf before baking for a slightly sweet, shiny crust.

9. **Bake:**
    - Bake for 30-35 minutes, or until the bread is golden brown and sounds hollow when tapped on the bottom.

10. **Cool:**
    - Allow the bread to cool in the pan for 10 minutes, then transfer to a wire rack to cool completely before slicing.

Tips:

- **Mint:** Fresh mint gives a more vibrant flavor, but dried mint works well too.
- **Flavor Variations:** For a different twist, you can also add a bit of lemon zest or a sprinkle of sea salt on top before baking.

Pfefferminzbrot adds a fresh and aromatic touch to any meal, making it a wonderful choice for those who enjoy unique flavors in their bread. Enjoy your homemade mint bread!

Joghurtbrot

Ingredients:

- **For the Dough:**
    - 2 1/2 cups all-purpose flour
    - 1 cup plain Greek yogurt (or regular plain yogurt)
    - 1/2 cup warm water (110°F or 45°C)
    - 2 teaspoons active dry yeast (or 1 packet)
    - 2 tablespoons honey or sugar
    - 1/4 cup olive oil or melted butter
    - 1 teaspoon salt

Instructions:

1. **Prepare the Yeast Mixture:**
    - In a small bowl, combine warm water and honey (or sugar). Stir to dissolve.
    - Sprinkle the yeast over the mixture and let it sit for 5-10 minutes, until frothy.
2. **Mix the Dough:**
    - In a large bowl, combine flour and salt.
    - Add the yeast mixture, yogurt, and olive oil (or melted butter) to the flour. Mix until a dough forms.
3. **Knead the Dough:**
    - Turn the dough onto a floured surface and knead for about 8-10 minutes, until smooth and elastic.
4. **First Rise:**
    - Place the dough in a lightly oiled bowl, cover with a cloth or plastic wrap, and let it rise in a warm, draft-free area for about 1-1.5 hours, or until doubled in size.
5. **Shape the Loaf:**
    - Punch down the dough and turn it out onto a floured surface.
    - Shape the dough into a loaf and place it in a greased 9x5-inch loaf pan or on a parchment-lined baking sheet.
6. **Second Rise:**
    - Cover the loaf and let it rise for another 30-45 minutes, or until puffy.
7. **Preheat the Oven:**
    - Preheat your oven to 375°F (190°C).
8. **Bake:**
    - Bake for 30-35 minutes, or until the bread is golden brown and sounds hollow when tapped on the bottom.
9. **Cool:**
    - Allow the bread to cool in the pan for 10 minutes, then transfer to a wire rack to cool completely before slicing.

Tips:

- **Yogurt Type:** Greek yogurt makes the bread extra moist and tender. Regular yogurt works well too but may make the dough a bit softer.
- **Flavor Variations:** Add herbs or spices to the dough for additional flavor.

Joghurtbrot is perfect for sandwiches, toast, or just with a bit of butter. Enjoy the light, fluffy texture and subtle tanginess of this delightful bread!

Zuckerrübensirupbrot

Ingredients:

- **For the Dough:**
    - 3 cups all-purpose flour
    - 1 cup whole wheat flour
    - 1/2 cup sugar beet syrup (or molasses as a substitute)
    - 1 1/2 cups warm water (110°F or 45°C)
    - 2 teaspoons active dry yeast (or 1 packet)
    - 1/4 cup vegetable oil or melted butter
    - 1 1/2 teaspoons salt
    - 1 teaspoon ground caraway seeds (optional)

Instructions:

1. **Prepare the Yeast Mixture:**
    - In a small bowl, combine warm water and a pinch of sugar. Stir to dissolve.
    - Sprinkle the yeast over the mixture and let it sit for 5-10 minutes, until frothy.
2. **Mix the Dough:**
    - In a large bowl, combine all-purpose flour, whole wheat flour, salt, and caraway seeds if using.
    - Add the yeast mixture, sugar beet syrup, and oil (or melted butter). Mix until a dough forms.
3. **Knead the Dough:**
    - Turn the dough onto a floured surface and knead for about 8-10 minutes, until smooth and elastic.
4. **First Rise:**
    - Place the dough in a lightly oiled bowl, cover with a cloth or plastic wrap, and let it rise in a warm, draft-free area for about 1-1.5 hours, or until doubled in size.
5. **Shape the Loaf:**
    - Punch down the dough and turn it out onto a floured surface.
    - Shape the dough into a loaf and place it in a greased 9x5-inch loaf pan or on a parchment-lined baking sheet.
6. **Second Rise:**
    - Cover the loaf and let it rise for another 30-45 minutes, or until puffy.
7. **Preheat the Oven:**
    - Preheat your oven to 375°F (190°C).
8. **Bake:**
    - Bake for 35-45 minutes, or until the bread is golden brown and sounds hollow when tapped on the bottom.
9. **Cool:**

- Allow the bread to cool in the pan for 10 minutes, then transfer to a wire rack to cool completely before slicing.

Tips:

- **Syrup:** Sugar beet syrup adds a unique, deep flavor. If unavailable, molasses is a suitable substitute but may alter the flavor slightly.
- **Texture:** For a denser bread, you can use more whole wheat flour or add seeds.

Zuckerrübensirupbrot is perfect for hearty sandwiches or simply enjoyed with a bit of butter. Enjoy the rich, slightly sweet flavor of this distinctive bread!

Osterbrot

Ingredients:

- **For the Dough:**
    - 4 cups all-purpose flour
    - 1/2 cup sugar
    - 1 teaspoon salt
    - 1 package (2 1/4 teaspoons) active dry yeast
    - 1 cup milk
    - 1/4 cup unsalted butter
    - 3 large eggs
    - 1 teaspoon vanilla extract
    - Zest of 1 lemon (optional)
    - 1/2 teaspoon ground cinnamon (optional)
- **For the Glaze:**
    - 1 egg, beaten
    - 1 tablespoon milk
- **For Decoration (optional):**
    - Colored sprinkles or sugar
    - 4-6 dyed Easter eggs (optional, for traditional decoration)

Instructions:

1. **Prepare the Yeast Mixture:**
    - In a small bowl, warm the milk to about 110°F (45°C). Stir in 1 tablespoon of sugar.
    - Sprinkle the yeast over the milk and let it sit for 5-10 minutes, until frothy.
2. **Mix the Dough:**
    - In a large bowl, combine flour, remaining sugar, salt, and cinnamon if using.
    - In another bowl, beat together the eggs, melted butter, and vanilla extract.
    - Add the yeast mixture and egg mixture to the dry ingredients. Mix until a dough forms.
3. **Knead the Dough:**
    - Turn the dough onto a floured surface and knead for about 8-10 minutes, until smooth and elastic.
4. **First Rise:**
    - Place the dough in a lightly oiled bowl, cover with a cloth or plastic wrap, and let it rise in a warm, draft-free area for about 1-1.5 hours, or until doubled in size.
5. **Shape the Loaf:**
    - Punch down the dough and turn it out onto a floured surface.

- Divide the dough into 3 equal pieces. Roll each piece into a long rope and braid the ropes together to form a loaf.
- Place the braided loaf on a parchment-lined baking sheet or in a greased loaf pan.

6. **Second Rise:**
    - Cover the loaf and let it rise for another 30-45 minutes, or until puffy.
7. **Preheat the Oven:**
    - Preheat your oven to 350°F (175°C).
8. **Prepare the Glaze:**
    - Brush the beaten egg mixed with milk over the surface of the loaf. This gives the bread a golden, shiny finish.
    - Sprinkle with colored sugar or sprinkles if desired.
9. **Bake:**
    - Bake for 30-35 minutes, or until the bread is golden brown and sounds hollow when tapped on the bottom.
10. **Cool:**
    - Allow the bread to cool on a wire rack before slicing.

Decoration (Optional):

- **Traditional Decoration:** If using dyed Easter eggs, gently press them into the dough before the second rise so they stay in place during baking.

Tips:

- **Flavor Variations:** Add raisins, currants, or chopped nuts for extra flavor and texture.
- **Sweetness:** Adjust the amount of sugar according to your taste preference.

Osterbrot is perfect for celebrating Easter with its festive appearance and delicious taste. Enjoy this special bread with butter, jam, or as part of your Easter meal!

Apfel-Zimt-Brot

Ingredients:

- **For the Dough:**
    - 2 1/2 cups all-purpose flour
    - 1/2 cup sugar
    - 1 teaspoon salt
    - 2 teaspoons ground cinnamon
    - 2 teaspoons baking powder
    - 1/2 teaspoon baking soda
    - 1/2 cup unsalted butter, softened
    - 2 large eggs
    - 1 cup milk
    - 1 teaspoon vanilla extract
    - 1 cup apples, peeled, cored, and chopped (about 1 medium apple)
- **For the Topping (optional):**
    - 2 tablespoons sugar
    - 1 teaspoon ground cinnamon

Instructions:

1. **Preheat the Oven:**
    - Preheat your oven to 350°F (175°C).
    - Grease and flour a 9x5-inch loaf pan or line it with parchment paper.
2. **Mix Dry Ingredients:**
    - In a medium bowl, whisk together flour, sugar, salt, cinnamon, baking powder, and baking soda.
3. **Cream Butter and Eggs:**
    - In a large bowl, beat the softened butter until creamy.
    - Add the eggs one at a time, beating well after each addition.
    - Stir in the vanilla extract.
4. **Combine Ingredients:**
    - Gradually add the dry ingredients to the butter mixture, alternating with milk. Mix until just combined.
    - Gently fold in the chopped apples.
5. **Transfer to Pan:**
    - Pour the batter into the prepared loaf pan and smooth the top with a spatula.
6. **Prepare Topping (optional):**
    - In a small bowl, mix sugar and cinnamon.
    - Sprinkle the mixture evenly over the top of the batter.
7. **Bake:**

- Bake for 50-60 minutes, or until a toothpick inserted into the center comes out clean and the top is golden brown.
8. **Cool:**
    - Allow the bread to cool in the pan for 10 minutes, then transfer to a wire rack to cool completely before slicing.

Tips:

- **Apples:** Use firm apples like Granny Smith or Honeycrisp for the best texture. Make sure to chop them into small pieces so they distribute evenly throughout the bread.
- **Moisture:** If you prefer a moister bread, you can increase the amount of apple slightly or add a tablespoon of apple sauce to the batter.
- **Add-Ins:** For extra flavor, consider adding chopped nuts or raisins to the batter.

Apfel-Zimt-Brot combines the comforting flavors of apples and cinnamon in a tender loaf that's sure to be a hit with family and friends. Enjoy your homemade apple cinnamon bread!

Essigbrot

Ingredients:

- **For the Dough:**
    - 3 1/2 cups all-purpose flour
    - 1 1/2 teaspoons salt
    - 1 tablespoon sugar
    - 2 teaspoons active dry yeast (or 1 packet)
    - 1 cup warm water (110°F or 45°C)
    - 1/4 cup vinegar (apple cider vinegar or white vinegar)
    - 2 tablespoons olive oil

Instructions:

1. **Prepare the Yeast Mixture:**
    - In a small bowl, combine warm water and sugar. Stir to dissolve.
    - Sprinkle the yeast over the mixture and let it sit for 5-10 minutes, until frothy.
2. **Mix the Dough:**
    - In a large bowl, combine flour and salt.
    - Add the yeast mixture, vinegar, and olive oil. Mix until a dough forms.
3. **Knead the Dough:**
    - Turn the dough onto a floured surface and knead for about 8-10 minutes, until smooth and elastic.
4. **First Rise:**
    - Place the dough in a lightly oiled bowl, cover with a cloth or plastic wrap, and let it rise in a warm, draft-free area for about 1-1.5 hours, or until doubled in size.
5. **Shape the Loaf:**
    - Punch down the dough and turn it out onto a floured surface.
    - Shape the dough into a loaf and place it in a greased 9x5-inch loaf pan or on a parchment-lined baking sheet.
6. **Second Rise:**
    - Cover the loaf and let it rise for another 30-45 minutes, or until puffy.
7. **Preheat the Oven:**
    - Preheat your oven to 375°F (190°C).
8. **Bake:**
    - Bake for 30-35 minutes, or until the bread is golden brown and sounds hollow when tapped on the bottom.
9. **Cool:**
    - Allow the bread to cool in the pan for 10 minutes, then transfer to a wire rack to cool completely before slicing.

Tips:

- **Vinegar:** The vinegar adds a subtle tanginess. If you prefer a milder flavor, you can reduce the amount slightly.
- **Texture:** This bread will have a slightly denser crumb due to the vinegar but will be wonderfully flavorful.

Essigbrot pairs well with a variety of toppings, from cheeses to meats, and makes a unique addition to any bread basket. Enjoy your tangy, homemade bread!

Kürbisbrot

Ingredients:

- **For the Dough:**
    - 2 1/2 cups all-purpose flour
    - 1 cup canned pumpkin (not pumpkin pie filling)
    - 1/2 cup sugar
    - 1/2 cup brown sugar
    - 1/2 cup vegetable oil or melted butter
    - 2 large eggs
    - 1/2 cup milk
    - 1 teaspoon vanilla extract
    - 1 teaspoon ground cinnamon
    - 1/2 teaspoon ground nutmeg
    - 1/2 teaspoon baking soda
    - 1 1/2 teaspoons baking powder
    - 1/2 teaspoon salt
    - 1/2 cup chopped nuts or chocolate chips (optional)

Instructions:

1. **Preheat the Oven:**
    - Preheat your oven to 350°F (175°C).
    - Grease and flour a 9x5-inch loaf pan or line it with parchment paper.
2. **Mix Dry Ingredients:**
    - In a medium bowl, whisk together flour, cinnamon, nutmeg, baking soda, baking powder, and salt.
3. **Mix Wet Ingredients:**
    - In a large bowl, whisk together pumpkin, sugar, brown sugar, oil (or melted butter), eggs, milk, and vanilla extract until smooth and well combined.
4. **Combine Ingredients:**
    - Gradually add the dry ingredients to the wet ingredients, mixing just until combined. Be careful not to overmix.
    - Fold in nuts or chocolate chips if using.
5. **Transfer to Pan:**
    - Pour the batter into the prepared loaf pan and smooth the top with a spatula.
6. **Bake:**
    - Bake for 50-60 minutes, or until a toothpick inserted into the center comes out clean and the bread is golden brown on top.
7. **Cool:**

- Allow the bread to cool in the pan for about 10 minutes, then transfer to a wire rack to cool completely before slicing.

Tips:

- **Pumpkin:** Make sure to use pure pumpkin puree, not pumpkin pie filling, as the latter contains added spices and sweeteners.
- **Texture:** For a slightly different texture, you can substitute half of the all-purpose flour with whole wheat flour.
- **Spices:** Adjust the amount of cinnamon and nutmeg to your taste or add other spices like cloves or ginger for extra flavor.

Kürbisbrot is perfect for breakfast, a snack, or as a dessert. Enjoy the rich, spiced flavor of this comforting bread!

Rosinenbrot

Ingredients:

- **For the Dough:**
    - 3 1/2 cups all-purpose flour
    - 1/4 cup sugar
    - 1 teaspoon salt
    - 2 teaspoons ground cinnamon
    - 2 teaspoons active dry yeast (or 1 packet)
    - 1 cup warm milk (110°F or 45°C)
    - 1/4 cup unsalted butter, melted
    - 2 large eggs
    - 1 cup raisins
- **For the Glaze (optional):**
    - 1 tablespoon milk
    - 1 tablespoon sugar

Instructions:

1. **Prepare the Yeast Mixture:**
    - In a small bowl, combine warm milk and sugar. Stir to dissolve.
    - Sprinkle the yeast over the milk mixture and let it sit for 5-10 minutes, until frothy.
2. **Mix the Dough:**
    - In a large bowl, whisk together flour, salt, and cinnamon.
    - Add the yeast mixture, melted butter, and eggs. Mix until a dough forms.
3. **Knead the Dough:**
    - Turn the dough onto a floured surface and knead for about 8-10 minutes, until smooth and elastic.
    - Fold in the raisins during the last few minutes of kneading.
4. **First Rise:**
    - Place the dough in a lightly oiled bowl, cover with a cloth or plastic wrap, and let it rise in a warm, draft-free area for about 1-1.5 hours, or until doubled in size.
5. **Shape the Loaf:**
    - Punch down the dough and turn it out onto a floured surface.
    - Shape the dough into a loaf and place it in a greased 9x5-inch loaf pan or on a parchment-lined baking sheet.
6. **Second Rise:**
    - Cover the loaf and let it rise for another 30-45 minutes, or until puffy.
7. **Preheat the Oven:**
    - Preheat your oven to 350°F (175°C).
8. **Prepare the Glaze (optional):**

        - Mix milk and sugar in a small bowl.
        - Brush the mixture over the top of the loaf before baking for a slightly sweet, shiny crust.
9. **Bake:**
        - Bake for 30-35 minutes, or until the bread is golden brown and sounds hollow when tapped on the bottom.
10. **Cool:**
        - Allow the bread to cool in the pan for 10 minutes, then transfer to a wire rack to cool completely before slicing.

Tips:

- **Raisins:** You can soak the raisins in warm water for 10 minutes before adding them to the dough to make them plumper and juicier.
- **Spices:** Adjust the amount of cinnamon or add other spices like nutmeg or cloves if desired.

Rosinenbrot is delicious on its own or with a bit of butter. Enjoy the sweet and spiced flavor of this homemade bread!

www.ingramcontent.com/pod-product-compliance
Lightning Source LLC
LaVergne TN
LVHW081604060526
838201LV00054B/2062